Ian Halperin is an international bestselling author and journalist who specialises in undercover investigations of the pop-culture world. His book *Shut Up and Smile*, an exposé of the world of fashion, was named Book of the Year in 2002 by Jackie Collins and his last work, *Love and Death: The Murder of Kurt Cobain*, was a *New York Times* bestseller.

HOLLYWOOD
Undercover

Revealing the Sordid
Secrets of Tinseltown

IAN HALPERIN

MAINSTREAM
PUBLISHING

EDINBURGH AND LONDON

This edition, 2008

First published in Great Britain in 2007 by
MAINSTREAM PUBLISHING COMPANY
(EDINBURGH) LTD
7 Albany Street
Edinburgh EH1 3UG

ISBN 9781845963217

A catalogue record for this book is available
from the British Library

Typeset in Garamond and Helvetica

Printed in Great Britain by
CPI Cox and Wyman, Reading, RG1 8EX

To my late mother, Miriam,
for whom I promised to win an Oscar

★ Acknowledgements ★

Thanks to the many brave people in the film industry who spoke on the record without fear of being blacklisted in Hollywood. I have changed the names of many people in the book who were not, understandably, willing to take the same risk. To Bill Campbell at Mainstream for believing in this project. Special thanks to everyone else at Mainstream who worked on this, especially Ailsa Bathgate and Graeme Blaikie.

Enormous thanks to my long-time writing partner, Max Wallace, who was in a coma with pneumonia for much of this but bounced back to help with editing and direction.

And to everyone who helped me along the way, including: Dr J.P. Pawliw Fry, Stuart Nulman, Clover Sky, Aldon James, Bob Luke, Danny Rossner, Kris Kostov, Vanessa and Karin, Jennifer Campbell, Joe Franklin, Jon Reisler, Mark Fleming, Luiza Barteledes, Adam Roebuck, David Gavrilchuk, Ron Deckelbaum, Julius Grey, Bob Shuman, Jackie Collins, Rebecca Williams, Nuno, Angie and Christine in Austin, Barbara Oshikoff, Colin Jefferson, Minelle Mahtani, Jeremy Morrison, Peter Santos, Audi Gozlan, Chaim Schwartz, Nate Colbert, Jose, Carl T, Alastair Sutherland, One Beyond, Terry Cullen, P. Diddy, George Karalias, Bill Brownstein, Walt Frasier, Shimon Datan, Tom Ellis, Amy Spragoo, Nikki Cargill, Nicola, Michael Friedlieb, Joey Reynolds, Mike Cohen, Nathan Myers and Paulo Santana.

★ Contents ★

★ Bringing the Book to Life ★

Hollywood Undercover allows the reader a whole new dimension
– video footage of all the key scenes, designed to bring the narrative
to life. Each time the word YouTube appears in brackets, simply go
to YouTube.com and enter the words 'His Highness Halperin' in the
search box, and either add in key words from that particular section
of the narrative to narrow down the search or surf through the list
of clips for footage of your favourite scenes.

For the avoidance of doubt, YouTube is solely a means of
viewing the footage and is not in any way associated with *Hollywood
Undercover.*

PROLOGUE

★ Hollywood Hex ★

It started as an assignment for Canada's largest TV network, CTV. Head to Los Angeles and film a documentary about aspiring Canadian actors trying to make it in Hollywood during 'pilot season', the period when producers develop and shoot hundreds of pilots, hoping they will be picked up by a television network and turned into a regular series. My task was simple enough, except for two not-so-small obstacles.

First, I had absolutely no experience producing films, for television or otherwise. I was alternately a journalist and a musician, depending on my mood and my desire to eat, and I couldn't see how either of these professions remotely qualified me to direct a documentary. It's true that I had once worked as a consultant for Britain's most famous documentary film-maker, Nick Broomfield, whose BBC film *Kurt & Courtney* was loosely based on one of my books. But the sum total of my experience on that film was being dragged from location to location by Broomfield as I watched him do his stuff, ambushing unsuspecting victims and making them look foolish. The lesson I had taken away from the project was that documentary film-making actually took talent and experience. However, my commissioning producer insisted that I was indeed the right person for the job because he had read my 2002 exposé, *Shut Up and Smile*, in which I had posed undercover as a male model and infiltrated the world of fashion. The book caused a bit of a stir in the industry and Jackie Collins had named it Book of the Year in the *Daily Mail*.

The producer believed I could 'blow the lid off' Hollywood in the same way I had the world of fashion.

Which brings me to the second obstacle. I knew even less about Hollywood than I did about making documentaries. The truth is I had just never really seen the point of movies and didn't go to very many of them, though I must admit there were a few that I loved. My friends insisted that films were a great escape, but when I wanted to escape I would put on a record by Miles Davis or John Coltrane. When I made the effort to see a film in a movie theatre, I usually thought it was a waste of time – two hours of my life that I would never get back. Perhaps it stems from my childhood when, like all Jews, my parents forced me to watch *The Ten Commandments* on television every Easter. There's nothing like three hours of Charlton Heston pretending to be moral to turn you off cinema for life.

Perhaps the pinnacle of my ignorance about Hollywood came one day in the mid-'80s when I was living in London. I had just finished busking close by and was sitting on a bench in Hyde Park reading the newspaper. An older woman came by with her dog and sat down beside me, eyed my saxophone case and then said, in an American accent, 'You're a musician. What kind of music do you play?'

'A little jazz,' I replied.

Without missing a beat, she responded, 'Oh, I used to be married to a couple of jazz musicians.'

'Really? Who?' I enquired innocently.

'Artie Shaw and Frank Sinatra,' came her reply.

I suppose somebody a little better versed in pop-culture history would have already known the answer to my next question, but I hadn't a clue.

'Are you serious? Who are you?'

She didn't seem at all surprised by my ignorance, but she was just a little taken aback when I didn't show more excitement at the answer. 'My name's Ava Gardner.'

Now, in all fairness, I had heard the name before and vaguely knew that she was somebody famous, but that's about it. I was definitely a little excited, but only because of her association with Sinatra. Next thing I knew, she was inviting me up to her apartment in nearby Hyde Park Towers for tea.

I later read that she was once considered among the most beautiful women in the world – 'face of an angel, body of a goddess', they said. But by the time I met her, she had suffered some health problems, leaving her with only a vestige of her legendary beauty. And that's not all that had happened to her face.

'You see this?' she said one day, pointing to a tiny scar above her lip, just visible beneath her make-up. 'That's where Frank kicked me after a drunken rampage.' By then, she had already told me a number of stories about Ol' Blue Eyes, none of them flattering (unless you count her declaration that he was 'hung like a mule'). Years later, I heard a rumour that Sinatra had once caught Ava in bed with Lana Turner and was out of his mind with rage. I wondered whether this incident could have given birth to the scar.

The most surprising of her stories was her explanation of how she had ended up living in England. 'It wasn't my idea,' she said matter-of-factly, then recounted how Frank's 'boys' had made it clear to her years earlier that it would be in her best interests to move across the Atlantic. 'Apparently he couldn't even handle living on the same continent as me,' she said. 'That's how jealous he still was because I left him.'

I wanted to know, did he threaten her?

'Not per se. It was his people who told me he wanted me gone, never him. But they were very persuasive, and I knew a lot of first-hand stories about what happened to people who crossed Frank. I wasn't about to take any chances.'

'Were they Mob?' I asked naively.

'What do you think?' she replied, as if I was a halfwit.

She told me lots more stories about Hollywood figures, along with juicy gossip that would have come in very handy for this book. But unfortunately I had barely heard of most of the people she dished dirt on, so the stories were wasted on me. One of her friends that I had definitely heard of, and who was practically her neighbour, was a certain lady with a palace across the park. It seemed that Ava and the Queen shared a passion for corgis and occasionally got together for dog-talk. 'She's very nice. Not at all what you'd expect. And do you want to know a secret that many Britons would kill to know?' she asked, excitedly. 'You'll never guess what she keeps in those giant purses of hers – little biscuits for the corgis! Isn't that funny?'

Even more interesting, she also told me that she believed the Queen despised Margaret Thatcher, who was Prime Minister at the time. To my surprise, she said Liz was apparently very worried by Thatcher's support of the apartheid regime in South Africa, which she believed was tearing apart the Commonwealth. Ava herself was deeply committed to the anti-apartheid cause. She said South Africa was the most beautiful country in the world and that she'd love to retire there, but she wouldn't set foot in the country until Mandela was free. She told me stories about growing up in the American South at the height of segregation and it was obvious that racism deeply troubled her. Just before I left England, she even financed an anti-apartheid benefit I organised at the Brixton Café.

All in all, I got the impression that Ava was a very lonely woman. Yet she didn't seem to miss the glamorous life she had once known. I was already living back in Canada when she died in 1990, having never fully recovered from a major stroke that had kept her bedridden for more than a year.

Even though I didn't know a whole hell of a lot about Hollywood when I began my journey, I was pretty certain that it was a very different town than the one over which Ava Gardner had reigned 50 years earlier. I also suspected that I wouldn't be welcomed quite as warmly as she had been.

Four days before I was scheduled to head to LA for the first phase of filming, I faced a further problem. Normally the production company arranges a crew – cameraman, soundman and production manager at the very least – but I had negotiated an unusual arrangement with the company who had contracted with CTV to deliver the documentary. Because the film was being shot almost exclusively in the United States, there were problems with bringing a Canadian crew over the border as a result of labour laws designed to protect American film jobs. In other words, a Canadian couldn't be hired to work in the US as long as there was a qualified American to do the job. So I had agreed to take a chunk of extra money and hire my own crew in the States, which meant I was responsible for their meals and accommodation as well. But I was so busy working on a feature story I had been assigned on New York's fine-dining industry that I had forgotten to hire the crew.

On the last day of my trip, I happened to be outside the Ed Sullivan Theater, where the David Letterman show is produced, watching that night's guests roll in at the side entrance on 53rd Street. I noticed a tall black guy with headphones on and a digital camera. He looked pretty cool, so I went up to him and asked what he was shooting. He introduced himself as Miles and explained that he had been hired by that night's musical guest, the roots soul phenomenon Cody Chesnutt, to shoot a behind-the-scenes documentary about touring with him. I told Miles I liked his style. I asked him where he was from and he replied LA. Bingo!

Better yet, he did his own sound and owned a camera, so my overheads would be significantly reduced.

I asked Miles when he'd be back in LA. 'In four days,' he replied. Which was exactly when he reported to the set of my film for his first day of work.

- ★ -

I arrive in Los Angeles without a plan and without a clue. I have been here a number of times before to promote my books, but that usually involved getting picked up at the airport by a driver and deposited in a four-star hotel. Now I am on my own, expected to navigate the Hollywood jungle.

I am travelling light, with just a case of blank mini-DV tapes, releases for everyone to sign, a couple of changes of clothes, my saxophone and a pair of rollerblades.

When I take the shuttle to the car rental firm to pick up the vehicle I have booked, an economy Dodge Stratus, I am not relishing the idea of spending a few months cramped into a sardine can with my 6 ft 8 cameraman and his equipment. I figure being in the film business must have some perks, so I sweet-talk my way to an upgrade by convincing the manager – a woman with cleavage down to the floor, practically dripping with silicone – that the vehicle I rent will be featured prominently in the film I am producing. I'm not actually sure how she thinks this will benefit her establishment, but five minutes later I cruise away in a shiny silver Dodge Durango SUV.

On the way to my hotel, I stop off at Mel's Drive-In on Sunset Boulevard. I have come here because it was the setting for *American Graffiti*, one of the few films I love. When the waitress approaches, the first thing I can't help notice is her boob job. Wow! I feel like I'm in Silicon Valley, not Hollywood. They serve an all-day breakfast at Mel's and when I order my eggs sunny-side up even they arrive looking inflated. To top it all off, an attractive black woman pulls up and sits in the next booth clearly sporting fake boobs as well. When she orders, I notice her deep voice. Then I look up and spot her Adam's apple. I have been in LA less than an hour and, so far, everything has been fake.

When I arrive at the Roosevelt Hotel, a majestic old hotel located on Hollywood Boulevard, the first thing I notice in their lobby is a statue of Charlie Chaplin. The way he is looking at me, he seems to know that I don't belong in his town.

Soon after checking in, the concierge informs me that the hotel is haunted, so I'd better watch my step. I laugh, but she appears to be completely serious. When I tell her I am doing a documentary about Hollywood, she insists on giving me a haunted tour of the place. (YouTube)

She informs me that one of the hotel's most frequent guests was Marilyn Monroe, who actually posed on the hotel's diving board in her first ever ad, for suntan lotion, before she was discovered as an actress. For years after she died, guests reported seeing Marilyn's image in the full-length mirror that hung in her poolside suite, Cabana 246. She shows me the mirror, which is now hung beside the lobby elevators. (Note to myself: leave instructions in my will to have my children call the *Hollywood Reporter* a few weeks after my death, notifying them of the ghostly image of Ian Halperin they saw in the mirror of the room I stayed in.)

Another common ghost-sighting, she tells me, is that of the actor Montgomery Clift, who she says still haunts suite 928, where he used to pace the halls back in 1953, memorising his lines while he was filming *From Here to Eternity* with Frank Sinatra. There are frequent reports of loud, eerie noises coming from the empty suite and of phones left mysteriously off the hook.

After a good night's sleep, my first order of business is finding some characters for my film. Throw a stone from any street corner in LA and if it misses a hooker it will likely hit a starving actor, but I have absolutely no idea how to differentiate an American from a Canadian. So I place an ad on Craig's List, a free Internet site that hooks people up.

My first response is promising: an actor from Ontario named

Dan Di Julio, who landed a meaty role a few years back playing Dan Aykroyd in a TV movie about Gilda Radner called *It's Always Something*, which was filmed in Canada. Based on the success of that movie, he had decided to chuck it all in and move to Los Angeles, assuming his Aykroyd role would quickly open doors to other parts. It didn't quite work out the way he planned.

By the time I meet him, he has been in LA for almost a year and hasn't landed a single acting job. He is practically homeless, living in a seedy hostel populated by other aspiring actors. To survive, he occasionally plays in a semi-professional LA football league.

By day, I follow him to audition after audition, each ending in a typical rejection. But at night, he proves an invaluable tour guide to the Hollywood scene. As long as I am paying the tab, he is all too willing to bring me to the bars where I can find other Canadians for my documentary.

One evening, we are sitting in the Bungalow Club sipping Martinis. Next to us is a gorgeous woman, who turns out to be an aspiring actress named Kathy Gallin. She barely acknowledges us until Di Julio turns to her and tells her I am a big-time film producer. Next thing I know, she has invited me to her pad and plied me with shots of vodka. I wake up the next morning completely naked in her bed, having apparently had sex with her, though I don't remember a thing. When she finds out I only make documentaries, she tells me, 'The only way to land a role in this town is to sleep with the producer, so I figured I'd just cut to the chase.'

Meanwhile, following Di Julio around, watching him fail time after time, is becoming more depressing, although it doesn't seem to deter him from his dream. In fact, he almost seems to regard being homeless as a rite of passage that precedes success, which he always feels is just around the corner.

'Look at Tom Hanks,' he tells me. 'He has already won the

Lifetime Achievement Award and he's not even 50. The guy's got a great career, yet I've heard him talk about how, when he finished his first TV show, *Bosom Buddies*, he spent the following year with no work and no opportunities and was even sleeping in his car at one point. In fact, the best opportunity he had, and he didn't even get it, was being considered for a yoghurt commercial. And look what happened to him.' (YouTube)

I didn't have the heart to break it to Di Julio that he was no Tom Hanks and was probably deluding himself by continuing to pursue a film career. The man had a dream and who was I to stomp on it? I figured Hollywood would eat him up and spit him out when it was good and ready.

And at least Di Julio had already landed a decent role. I definitely couldn't say the same thing for any of the other aspiring Canadian actors I followed to audition after audition. One of them, Carrie Simmons, tells me after yet another rejection, 'It's like a cattle call. You have 150 girls competing to get the casting director's attention and, you can imagine, it just sucks. You either say fuck this and give it up, or you kiss ass and hope it'll land you something.'

One acting coach I interviewed summed it up best. 'These kids come here because they're told, "You're the most beautiful kid in Saskatchewan." Big fucking deal! They're all the most beautiful person from wherever they come from. The ones who survive are the ones who have something extra.'

At least one of the actresses I follow, a woman from Canada named Melissa, saw the writing on the wall. Two weeks after I began filming her, she had already given up the dream and become a stripper.

I couldn't help but think of Marilyn Monroe's observation about this town: 'Hollywood is a place where they'll pay you $50,000 for a kiss and 50 cents for your soul.'

After weeks of this type of depressing story, one after another,

I realise my documentary is becoming a cliché. I desperately need a different angle.

Then it strikes me. I had posed undercover as a model a few years earlier to write my exposé of the fashion business, so why not take the same approach in Hollywood? I decide I will pose as an aspiring actor and infiltrate the movie business, thereby documenting an actor's life from the inside. But again the obstacles are obvious. Principally, the question of talent. If I have any, it certainly escaped the notice of my high-school drama teacher. I console myself that at least I have a leg-up on the competition – I don't need a day job as a waiter. And let's face it, if Johnny Knoxville can become a movie star, how hard can it be?

1

★ The Porn Superstar and the Supermodel ★

My favourite story about Hollywood involves the 1930s Mexican-American movie starlet Lupe Velez. In 1944, Lupe decided to kill herself, but, like the drama queen she was, she wanted to go out in style so that she would always be remembered. On the fateful day, she had her bedroom re-painted all in white. She got her hair and nails done. She had the room filled with flowers and her bed surrounded by lighted candles. And after taking a fistful of Seconal, she arranged herself on the bed so it would look like she was sleeping peacefully. She was wearing blue satin pyjamas. Unfortunately, the pills didn't mix well with the burritos she had consumed as her last meal. So, in a groggy state, she stumbled into the bathroom to throw up and that's where they eventually found her, with her head in the toilet. I couldn't help but think there was a cautionary tale there somewhere, but it wasn't going to deter me from my quest.

Not long after I started shooting my film, I received some devastating news. My mother, Miriam, had had a relapse of the cancer that was thought to be in remission. I flew back to Montreal to be with her. While I was there, I told her about the change of direction for my film and how I was going to be an actor. I promised her that I would win an Oscar and dedicate it to her. She died a few days later.

I returned to Los Angeles after the funeral, still shaken, but I remembered my promise to my mother and, though I wasn't deluded enough to think I would be winning any statues in the near future, I resolved to make a kick-ass documentary and dedicate it to my mom.

A couple of calls and I am put in touch with a well-known Hollywood manager who is kind enough to give me advice on how to get started. 'First, you get a top-drawer photographer to take some head-shots. You can't get an agent without a head-shot and you can't get an audition without an agent.'

Fortunately, even here, I have a leg-up on the competition. I'm hoping I can draw on one of my old fashion-industry contacts, the former supermodel Janice Dickinson, who is now a respected fashion photographer. I had read her book, *No Lifeguard on Duty*, which includes photo shoots of Madonna, Liam Neeson and Jack Nicholson. In addition, I figure, having dated a long list of movie stars, including Sylvester Stallone, Bruce Willis and Warren Beatty, Dickinson knows a thing or two about the real world of Hollywood. She would tell me what I needed to know.

Janice is amused when I call but agrees to shoot me. 'Dress in black,' she tells me. 'Head to toe.'

We are to meet at the Roosevelt. The hotel is such a majestic architectural gem, invoking the golden era of Hollywood, when stars were stars and I'd have been lucky to get a job as a janitor at Warner Brothers. The place itself is a Hollywood landmark and it was in its Blossom Room that the first Academy Awards were hosted in 1929. Before meeting Janice, I sneak in and stand right at its centre, trying to absorb the energy of the room and picture how it felt being there on that first Oscar night. When I exit, I pass the Chaplin statue and ask a passer-by to take a photo of me and Charlie. Staying at the Roosevelt is a crash course in the birth of the film business – an industry that reinvented how people spent their leisure time.

From the hotel lobby, Janice and I take the elevator to the balcony so that suddenly we are looking over the entire Hollywood skyline. She is all business. She backs me against the ledge and then begins fixing my hair, pushing it back with her fingers. Her strokes become slower and then she very delicately moves each strand to just where she wants it, designing the perfect look for my hair. She steps back and looks at the result.

'Stand straighter,' she tells me. 'No, not that straight. Relax, drop your shoulders.'

I look back at her to see if I have found the appropriate pose.

'Don't look at me for approval. Look inside your heart. Tell yourself you are the real deal and then show me that confidence. C'mon, exude it. Make me want to know what it is that makes you so damn confident.' She starts clicking away – click, click click, click click, non-stop.

'Force yourself on me. Make love to me. Make love to the camera. Kiss me, kiss the camera.' (YouTube)

I feel myself getting more into the shoot, eating up the encouragement – but part of me, a big part of me, is still wondering if this documentary isn't just one of those crazy ideas that never gets off the ground. Schwab's drugstore, where countless stars were discovered during Hollywood's heyday, no longer exists, but if I had whatever it took to make the movie moguls a buck, they'd have known where to look for me.

'You look great,' Janice says, breaking into my reverie. 'This is incredible.' And the more she says it, the more I start believing it. After all, this is a woman who calls herself the world's first supermodel, though I wonder what Twiggy would have to say to that. Still, she knows a thing or two about being on this side of the camera.

By the time the shoot is over, I am more than willing to believe that I am the most amazing subject she has ever shot.

'How was I?' I ask, wanting to soak up just a little bit more of her praise. 'It was great,' she answers. 'But let's see what the film tells us.'

Once again, she is all business.

That night, as reality hits me, I'm just praying that there will be one photo that will take me through the door.

A couple of days later, Janice leaves a message on my answering machine to meet her at the Roosevelt that afternoon. In the lobby, she takes out two or three photos. 'These are the ones you should use,' she tells me.

'What do I do next?' I ask her. 'Who should I get in touch with?'

She is all too glad to point me in the right direction. The photos, she says, should get a good agent interested in me. She also hands me an extensive list of contacts and tells me to use her name with each one.

'I don't need any great success, but I need to get some part – maybe even just a walk-on,' I confide in her. 'Do you think I have a chance?'

She seems impatient with my insecurity, giving me the 'are you for real?' look.

'Listen up, my friend,' she begins. 'A lot of successful actors these days have bloated egos, very little talent and even less brains. Take it from me, I've dated most of them. You'll do fine.'

I walk Janice to her black Mercedes SUV. Before she leaves she looks me in the eyes and gives me a kiss on the lips. I practically melt. Being kissed on the lips by the world's most notorious supermodel is better than meeting any Hollywood A-list actor; in fact, nothing remotely compares, not even meeting Oprah Winfrey, Princess Di or Woody Allen, three other celebrities I've met over the years.

Back in my hotel room, I open up the Yellow Pages and look under the heading 'Talent Agents'. I start cruising through the list. There is something very strange about the idea that you can look through the Yellow Pages and start a career that can make you an international celebrity. It's a bit like looking for a campaign manager who will make you President. But I go ahead and make the first call.

'I'm an aspiring actor looking for representation. I have a head-shot. Will you meet with me?'

To my amazement, the first one says, 'Come on over.' She gives me an appointment for the next day and I scribble the time in my diary, then move on to the next one. In the next hour or so, I call close to a dozen agents. Four or five give me appointments; the rest say, 'Send the head-shot and your info [height, weight, any previous acting experience] and we'll get back to you.' By the end of the day, I have made eight solid appointments but decide I will show up at four or five, figuring by then I'll know what I need to know about how the agents work.

As I prepare for my first meeting the next day, I realise I have to paste my name and résumé on the back of each head-shot. And then it hits me. I can't very well use my real name. Someone may recognise it, especially since my last book, *Love and Death*, had recently hit the *New York Times* bestseller list. For *Shut Up and Smile*, I had chosen the pseudonym Alfred Edgar Neuman (of *Mad* magazine fame). The allusion not only went undetected but also landed me a professional modelling assignment for the Fubu clothing line. If I was going to remain incognito in Hollywood, I would need an equally suitable moniker — perhaps something a little less obvious, as surely movie types are a little more on the ball than the fashionistas. I eventually choose my new name after watching a rerun of the American sitcom *All in the Family*: M. Stivic, Archie Bunker's son-in-law, whom he refers to as 'Meathead'. I will be a modern Meathead taking on Hollywood.

As I enter the reception room at the first agency, dressed head to toe in black — figuring what works for Janice will work for everyone in Hollywood — I am struck by the fact that the walls are lined with head-shots. This is some successful agent, I tell myself. But then, as

I scan the walls, I cannot find one photo of anyone I even remotely recognise. Perhaps I missed one, I think, but before I get a chance to do a more thorough scan, a woman in her late 30s, a petite brunette, comes over and, all businesslike, asks for my head-shot. She takes it out of the envelope and, eyes wide open, head pulled back as if she cannot believe what her eyes are telling her, announces, 'You're going to be the next Kevin Spacey!'

'OK,' I say.

'You've just got it,' she says, shaking her head from side to side in disbelief. 'You really have. Come right into my office.'

As we sit opposite each other, she continues to lay it on thick. 'We'll definitely get you into casting directors' rooms. But you are going to have to follow certain procedures, such as getting a good acting coach.'

'Do you really think there are roles for guys like me?' I ask her. 'It seems you have to be no more than 20 years old to be cast in this town.'

'Oh no,' she says, with absolute certainty, then explains that being a bit older is to my advantage because I won't have to compete with the throng of teens descending on Hollywood.

Sounds good. Twenty minutes later, we are still talking. I finally ask her how she learns about new parts that open up and she tells me about the breakdowns, the daily list of auditions issued by the studios.

'So, I hope you sign up with us,' she says, pulling the meeting to a close. 'Oh, and there is a $1,000 registration fee that you have to pay.'

I tell her I'll have to think about it.

I have since learned that agents who believe in their own judgement don't ask for or take any sign-up fees. Don't go with an agent who asks you for money is my advice.

I discover over the months that there are indeed some very honest Hollywood agents. I meet up with one, named Richard Kerner, and ask him straight out: 'Do you think I have any chance of making it in this business?'

Before he can answer that question, he says, he must ask me several questions.

He gets down to business, enquiring about my previous acting experience. I tell him that I never even landed a role in my high-school play, though I was once cast as a flying monkey in an elementary-school production of *The Wizard of Oz*.

'Your communication skills?' he asks. 'Any experience doing any job that involved a lot of communication?' I tell him I hosted a local radio show in Montreal several years ago. He writes that down.

He also tells me that I will need an acting coach.

Finally, I present him with the head-shot that Janice took. He looks at me and says, 'You'll make it. If you work hard enough, you'll make it.'

Kerner, a native New Yorker, does not ask me for money and drops into the conversation that I should avoid any agent who does. He says normally he would not consider signing any actor over 21.

'In this town, if you're over 21 and don't have an agent, the reality is you'll never succeed. In your case, you have an original look, so if you make it I won't be surprised. But because of your age, the odds are certainly against you.'

Amazingly, no one ever asks me the question I am most nervous about, because I can't answer it honestly: why do you want to become an actor?

I get more daring in the next interview, telling the agent that I will sign with him only if he can guarantee me that within two years I'll have a chance to win an Oscar. I tell him I'm not in this for mediocrity but to reach the highest level.

He laughs, but answers the question quite seriously.

'Look, it's a very difficult thing to win an Oscar.'

'Have any of your previous clients been nominated for an Oscar?' I ask him.

'No,' he replies.

After four or five interviews, my feeling is that none of the agents really know what they are looking for. It seems that if you walk in and simply have a pulse, they are willing to take you seriously. I keep returning to something Kerner said: 'If I have twenty-five clients and one of them makes it, I'm rich.' It is a shit-against-the-wall kind of business. Whatever sticks, sticks. But I don't have time to wait around; I have only a few months to make my Hollywood career.

At the next agency I visit, a seedy storefront off Hollywood Boulevard, it seems I have struck paydirt. The agent tells me he can probably land me a number of roles, some of them shooting that week.

Unfortunately, each of them involves hardcore porn. And, although I fear I am not suitably endowed to take him up on the offers, I am intrigued.

Stepping out of my undercover persona, I reveal that I am a Canadian film-maker doing a documentary. I ask him how many aspiring actors turn to porn when their Hollywood dreams fail to materialise.

'More than you can count,' he says. He tells me that one out of a thousand actors who come to LA are successful. The rest either go back home or turn to stripping or porn to survive. 'You know who can enlighten you on this subject?' he says. 'Ron Jeremy.'

That's one movie actor I had definitely heard of. The legendary Jeremy is the most prolific male porn star in history. He has starred in almost two thousand X-rated features in a career spanning three decades. One phone call later, I have an appointment to meet Jeremy the next day at a Hollywood sex boutique.

Fifteen minutes before we are scheduled to meet, I have a

brainstorm. I approach what appears to be a hooker on Hollywood Boulevard, one of the classier of the girls plying their trade, and tell her that I'm about to meet up with Ron Jeremy. I figure he'll take me more seriously if I show up with a beautiful woman on my arm. Linda – who, it turns out, is more of a stripper than a hooker – eagerly agrees to accompany me. 'It's always been my dream to be in a film with him,' she says.

Jeremy's waiting for me when we arrive and, sure enough, he's impressed by my date. 'I heard a rumour you're not wearing any underwear,' he says to her before I can get a word in. 'Are you shaved?'

Finally, he turns to me and asks me what I want to know. I ask him how he got started in porn. To my surprise, he tells me that his porn career came about accidentally after years of teaching special education to disabled kids in New York. His first ambition was to be a mainstream movie actor.

'There's a lot of frustrated actors in the business, number one being me,' he says. 'I got my degree in the theatre, a Bachelor in theatre, and a Masters in special ed. I started my acting career doing off-Broadway plays in New York, but the job market for actors was horrible. I eventually quit teaching to chase theatre jobs, but, after a few years of not doing work, I was approached one day to do an adult movie. I thought it was kind of sleazy, but I figured, what the heck, at least it's a chance to perform after years of not getting any work. I told myself it's more like being an actor than a waiter's job, and then one thing led to another. At the time, a lot of the same directors were doing both mainstream and porn, and I just got into doing them side by side. I even consulted on *9½ Weeks*, with Mickey Rourke and Kim Basinger.' (YouTube)

'Was it difficult making the transition back and forth?' I ask him.

'Well, when your first scene is an eight-man interracial dwarf anal gang bang, it gets easier from there,' Jeremy answers with a straight face.

The closest he came to a steady mainstream acting job, he recalls, was in the '70s, when he did a TV pilot for director Roger Avery, which included a recurring role for Jeremy.

'All the executives are total idiots,' he says. 'They always green-light total crap and this was an intelligent project. NBC rejected it. They had no foresight.'

He says he still dreams of winning an Oscar. 'Will it ever happen? No. An Oscar Mayer wiener maybe. You're really limited if you do porn. It helps you in some places, hurts you in others. I've gotten mainstream work because of porn. I did a cameo as myself in a Dustin Hoffman film. But it hurts you with Disney, hurts you doing a TV commercial. "Hi, this is Ron Jeremy, for Ultrabrite . . ." Traci Lords made the transition successfully, but she had to denounce porn to do it.'

Despite an increasingly burgeoning and lucrative porn career, Jeremy confides that he has still never given up on his dream to be a mainstream Hollywood actor, citing one of the definite downsides of porn. 'It's very tough having a steady relationship when you're in porn,' he laments. 'You know, you have a bowl of cereal and you say, "OK, honey, I'm off to do five chicks. See ya Thursday." It's tough on a relationship.' (YouTube)

It's difficult getting Jeremy to pay attention to my questions, as he's busy fondling my stripper. 'We just met, she's a cutie,' he tells me. 'I want to go in a car with her.' I ask him if he thinks she could break into the business.

'Well, you know, a lot of girls aspire to do porn these days. I don't really endorse porn for people,' he says. 'You get some pissed off father, brother, uncle, cousin, next-door neighbour, piano teacher, gardener mad at me. They'll ask the girl "Who made you get into the business?" and it will make me look like an asshole. They think porno people are walking around schoolyards recruiting girls. I've done this for 26 years, 1,700 movies, with everybody on the planet, so why should I take a chance on getting somebody pissed at me? I'd have to tell them, "Listen, putz, they came to me." It's just not worth it.'

'How has the business changed since you broke in?' I ask.

'In the old days, you felt like a real actor. You got a quarter of a million dollars for ten days of dialogue and one day of sex. Now when you go to work, you're having sex the minute you walk in the door. The dialogue is: "Here's a cup of coffee. Blow me."'

I finally ask him the question porn aficionados have been wanting to ask for years: why has a relatively unattractive, overweight, hairy guy like him – in his words, a 'schlub' – become the superstar of the porn world?

The answer is simple, he tells me. 'It's my schlong. I actually have a tattoo on my penis of a bigger penis.'

At that, the stripper lifts up her skirt to show Jeremy a tattoo of a *Playboy* bunny on her ass. I still haven't had a chance to ask him if he has any advice to help me land a (mainstream) acting role, but I am quickly aware the interview is over, as they head out to his car and speed off into the distance.

No closer to my goal, I am walking down the street one day when I see a poster for a free acting seminar promising Hollywood success: 'How to Get an Agent. How to Get Work', the poster shouts.

Why not? What do I have to lose? Little do I know when I arrive at the seminar that it is being conducted by the Church of Scientology, which I have a vague notion of being some sort of science-fiction cult-religion that is all the rage in Hollywood circles.

The seminar I attend takes place on Hollywood Boulevard and, in the half-hour session, the instructor explains the benefits of using Scientology to further one's acting career. There are about six of us in attendance at this introductory workshop and we are all pretty bored with the whole thing until the woman mentions several well-known members of the Church who she claims owe their success to Scientology. The names Tom Cruise, John Travolta, Mimi Rogers, Jenna Elfman and Kirstie Alley definitely catch our attention. She explains how supportive these actors are of the Church and how we too can enjoy success in Hollywood if only we follow the same path. Apparently, the Church runs a number of what they call 'celebrity centres' – retreats where well-known personalities take courses and where aspiring actors can also achieve enlightenment. The instructor passes out info on the history of the Church and its founder, L. Ron Hubbard, at one time also a bestselling science-fiction writer. It all looks pretty harmless.

At the end of the session, we get to ask questions. Everyone seems keen on joining except one woman, who asks if there's any chance that this process is used to brainwash us. I expect the instructor to deny it. Instead, she says it's important not to lose sight of the importance of attaining spirituality in LA, and Scientology is the best way to do that. I ask whether there are any fees to sign up and she says she can't give details at this point. After I press her, she finally admits there are some fees involved, but I'd only find out later on. This concerns me. To find out how much one has to pay, it seems you have to join first, then ask questions. A little dodgy, if you ask me.

I am determined to find out more. But when I take it upon myself to do a little research – which mostly consists of reading an investigative feature about Scientology that appeared in the *LA Times* – what I discover about the religion just confuses me.

The problem with trying to figure out what Scientology is all about, according to the *Times,* is that there is no one book, like the Koran or the Bible, that comprehensively sets forth the religion's beliefs. Instead, the Church's theology is found scattered among the many writings and speeches of its founder. And it appears to be no accident that a member can't simply open a book to discover the religion's revelations. Rather, the world according to Hubbard is revealed to members through a series of very expensive, and mostly secret, courses that take years to complete and can cost more than a hundred thousand dollars altogether.

The Church claims to have more than 6.5 million members throughout the world, but many religious experts maintain that the actual figure is considerably smaller. Whatever the membership, the *Times* claims that only a tiny fraction have ascended to the upper reaches. One Scientology publication, in fact, claims that fewer than 900 members have completed the Church's highest course, entitled 'Truth Revealed'. Most members start their education in Scientology by reading Hubbard's *Dianetics: The Modern Science of Mental Health*.

'To the uninitiated, Hubbard's theology would resemble pure science fiction, complete with galactic battles, interplanetary civilizations and tyrants who roam the universe,' writes the *Times*, which examined voluminous court records, Church documents and Hubbard speeches to glean clues about the religion.

I find out that at the core of the Scientology teachings is a belief in an immortal soul, or 'thetan', that passes from one body to the next through numerous reincarnations spanning trillions of years.

Over the years, Hubbard claimed to Church associates that he had been many different people before being born as Lafayette Ronald Hubbard on 13 March 1911 in Tilden, Nebraska. One of them was Cecil Rhodes, the British-born diamond king of southern Africa. Another, according to a former aide, was a marshal to Joan of Arc.

After Hubbard's death in 1986, a Scientology publication described him as 'the original musician', who three million years previously had invented music while going by the name Arpen Polo.

The publication noted that his first song was written 'a bit after the first tick of time'.

Hubbard realised that his accounts of past lives might sound suspect to outsiders, so he counselled his disciples to keep quiet. Hence the unprecedented secrecy surrounding the religion and its theology.

One of the most popular stories used to discredit the Church – repeated gleefully on the hundreds of anti-Scientology websites operated by former Scientologists and anti-cult organisations – is something Hubbard was supposed to have said shortly before he launched the Church. There are a number of versions of the story, but the long and the short of it is that he supposedly said that the easiest way to make a million was to start your own religion. It would be easy to assume that this is merely urban legend, or more likely a story concocted by Scientology's legion of opponents. But there appears to be considerable evidence that he did in fact say this, possibly on more than one occasion.

The evidence, though occasionally contradictory, comes from a number of witnesses who knew Hubbard and claim they heard him say this. The first is Sam Merwin, who in the 1940s was the editor of a science-fiction magazine called *Thrilling Wonder Stories*. In 1986, Merwin told an interviewer: 'I always knew [Hubbard] was exceedingly anxious to hit big money – he used to say he thought the best way to do it would be to start a cult.'

In the late 1940s, Hubbard had been invited to address the Eastern Science-Fiction Association, hosted by its director, sci-fi writer Sam Moskowitz, who later recalled the occasion. 'Hubbard spoke . . . I don't recall his exact words; but in effect, he told us that writing science fiction for about a penny a word was no way to make a living. If you really want to make a million, he said, the quickest way is to start your own religion.'

The Church denied this was said, calling upon two well-known science-fiction personalities who both claimed they also attended the same talk by Hubbard but didn't hear any such statement.

Even if Hubbard did say it, what the opponents of Scientology rarely acknowledge is that George Orwell had famously written something similar in 1938: 'But I have always thought there might be a lot of cash in starting a new religion . . .' Perhaps Hubbard simply thought Orwell's line was an amusing conversation starter.

Or perhaps not.

By the early 1970s, the religion that Hubbard had founded had indeed made him well over $1 million (some estimates say he had $650 million at the time of his death) and was becoming increasingly popular and powerful. This made a number of people nervous, including, apparently, the United States government.

During my research, I read that Hubbard had by now become paranoid and came up with a plan to erase from federal government files what he believed was false information being circulated to discredit him and the Church. He codenamed the plan Snow White. It would eventually land most of his top lieutenants in prison.

Lists of 'enemies' were compiled and they were subjected to smear campaigns and dirty tricks. The Guardian Office, responsible for legal affairs and investigations within the Church, targeted people in the government, the media, the medical profession or anybody who got in their way. One of the nastiest examples of its tactics was the dirty little campaign aimed at New York author Paulette Cooper whose 1972 exposé, *The Scandal of Scientology*, made her the Church's public enemy number one.

According to the *Times*, Cooper was framed on criminal charges by Guardian Office members, who forged bomb threats to the Church in her name. The FBI and its agents investigated Cooper, whose fingerprints matched those on the letter. Cooper was indicted by a grand jury for the bomb threats, as well as for lying under oath about her innocence. Two years later, with Cooper on the verge of suicide, her reputation destroyed, prosecutors finally dismissed the charges.

Today, the Church acknowledges Operation Snow White but maintains it was the work of renegade members who may have broken the law but who believed they were justified because of the government's long-standing harassment and persecution of Scientology.

So is it a different Church today than 30 years ago, as its members maintain? I was determined to find out.

I had recently hooked up with a Calvin Klein model/actress named Jennifer Holmes, who had starred in a film called *Jenifa* that was highly acclaimed in several foreign markets, including Japan. My friend Prentice Lennon had introduced me to Jennifer, telling me she'd be perfect for my film because she was an up-and-coming young actress who was already generating quite a buzz in Hollywood. I had been following her progress for my film and now I decide she is going to be my entrée to the world of Scientology. I place a call to the Church's main office, explaining that Jennifer recently appeared in a print ad with Brad Pitt, that she was on the verge of stardom and that she was interested in possibly joining the Church to help her achieve her goals. Could they possibly show her around? To my amazement, they ask if I can come by that afternoon. The next thing I know, Jennifer and I are being greeted at the gates of the LA celebrity centre – a magnificent Hollywood hotel/palace – by the centre's vice-president, Greg LeClaire. He is a little taken aback when he sees my video camera, but when I truthfully explain that I am doing a documentary following Jennifer's quest to make it in Hollywood, LeClaire not only agrees to be filmed but signs a release giving me permission to use the interview.

As he takes us on a tour, the charismatic LeClaire launches into a passionate commercial on the benefits of Scientology.

'Anybody can benefit from Scientology, whether you're eight years old or a hundred and eight,' he tells us. 'You can use it at any stage of your life. Scientology is a very practical religion. If you talk to members of the Church, they'll tell you it helps them attain happiness by overcoming obstacles. That's why it's so popular in the entertainment industry.' (YouTube)

He tells us that there are twelve celebrity centres like this one around the world, specifically geared towards artists. Jennifer asks him whether the Church caters for celebrities in the hope that they will spread the gospel and attract a lot of members. In other words, aren't they simply using these big-name actors?

He seems taken aback by the question. 'Well, I don't take it upon myself to speak for celebrities,' he says. 'The interesting thing about this is that because people benefit so much, they want to tell other people about it. It has fantastic word-of-mouth. When you hear a celebrity talking about it, they're not doing anything different than anybody else, they just have a bigger voice. The fact is that more than a million people every year take their first steps in Scientology.'

I can certainly see the appeal of celebrities for the Church, which is why Scientology seems to devote so much time, effort and money pandering to and pampering celebrities. But how does Scientology help an aspiring actor achieve success, as LeClaire has implied a number of times since we started talking?

'Well, the religion can be an especially positive influence when you try to make it in Hollywood, where there is a definite lack of morals,' he explains. 'There are drugs. There's promiscuity. And, you know, with religion, you basically have a broader purpose in life. And when you talk to people who have done Scientology, it really helps to overcome that.'

I can almost see his point, and want to press further, but I am suddenly distracted by a movement in the bushes. When I look closer, I realise there is a cameraman filming us, which results in the strange spectacle of our video cameras focusing on each other in a bizarre showdown. When I ask LeClaire what's going on, he seems a bit embarrassed, but has an explanation ready.

'He's just my guy, because we might use this someday, somehow,' he explains, as if it's the most natural thing in the world.

I had a ton of questions I still wanted to ask him concerning all the rumours I had read since attending the meeting. Is it true that Scientologist Lisa Marie Presley was encouraged by the Church to marry Michael Jackson in order to lure him and his vast fortune into the Church? For that matter, do they think Lisa Marie's father, Elvis – a devout Christian – would approve of the fact that his estate is practically being managed by the Church? And what about the persistent rumours that the so-called Church is in fact a cult which uses sophisticated brainwashing tactics to recruit members? But the guy in the bushes had creeped me out and I figure it is time to get the hell out of there. My questions, along with a much more troubling rumour that I would soon hear about the Church of Scientology, would have to wait for another day.

It was time to act on some advice that Janice Dickinson had recently given me. She told me that if I wanted to make it in Hollywood, I needed to sell myself.

'How do I do that?' I had asked her.

'Get yourself a publicist,' had been her reply.

'Don't they cost something like $50,000 a month?'

'Hey, if you want to make it, you can't be cheap,' she had answered, as if she expected me to pluck the necessary funds out of my ass.

Not to be deterred, I decided to put an ad on Craig's List for a publicist. Sure enough, I got exactly one reply, from an up-and-coming professional named Melanie Gideon, who had been working in the underground film scene and with a number of musicians. Ironically, it seemed like she was going to try to use me to take her own career to the next level. 'I've been looking for the right

Canadian to represent,' she told me at our first meeting. 'Canadians do well in Hollywood. I've been searching for my own Jim Carrey, Martin Short or John Candy. Stick with me and we'll both have mansions in the Hollywood Hills before you know it.'

I didn't want to disabuse her of these delusions and, besides, I liked her confidence, so I agreed to be her client, especially when she offered to work for a percentage of my acting salary instead of the usual flat fee.

Little did she know what was in store for her.

2

★ Queers of the Round Table ★

A week after I hired my new publicist, I was no closer to the elusive goal of landing a movie role and I was beginning to seriously toy with the idea of changing the focus of my documentary to a profile of Ron Jeremy and the LA porn industry. But Melanie assured me that she had a plan. She offered to take me to a Thursday night poker game in the Hollywood Hills where the participants are all employed in the film industry.

There was one small thing she wanted me to be aware of before I went: her friends were all flagrantly gay and called themselves the 'Queers of the Round Table'. In fact, to my surprise, she told me that one of the regular players was a well-known former sitcom star, though he wouldn't be there because he had a work commitment.

'They love to dish the dirt about Hollywood,' she said, warning me that I won't be able to bring my video camera, for obvious reasons.

When I arrive, I am greeted by the host, Karl, who works as a set designer. He tells me I'm welcome to play with them and that they will be glad to fill me in on 'this nasty town', but he does make one request: 'Don't get us into trouble.' I promise not to use real names, but that's not good enough. 'It's not so much *our* names we're worried about,' he explains. 'If we should just happen to spill a little gossip on an industry power-player or a famous actor, it might be better for you to keep your lips sealed. Oh, what the hell, to be honest I don't give a fuck who you tell, just don't let it get back to us!'

With the ground rules agreed, he introduces me to his friends: Lenny, who is a location scout for movies and TV shows, and Christopher, who is a script editor. None of them seems particularly light in the loafers, though it soon becomes apparent that this is no beer-and-nachos poker game. Karl offers me a choice of a green apple Martini or a Cosmopolitan, along with macadamia nuts, home-made cookies and smoked oysters. Already I am happy I came. But once the cocktails start flowing and the game gets under way – and, yes, the table is indeed round – I realise that I will get more out of this gathering than high-class hooch and hors d'oeuvres.

'So, you wanna know about Hollywood?' asks Lenny. 'Well, the town's a cesspool.'

Karl corrects him. 'More like a viper's pit!'

'So, why do you guys work here?' I ask.

'Because it's fabulous,' Lenny exclaims, seeming to contradict his last statement. 'The money's great, the perks are to die for and you get to meet famous people.'

'You mean you get to fuck famous people,' Karl pipes in.

'The only famous person I ever did was a guy from a Rolaids commercial,' Lenny replies.

'That's because you're butt ugly,' chimes Christopher to uproarious laughter around the table.

'Shut up, you mean old fag,' Lenny responds in a mock hurt tone.

This is already very entertaining, but I seize the moment to segue in something I've been dying to know. 'Speaking of famous people, is it true that [famous former sitcom actor] sometimes plays in your game?'

'Yeah, he's here almost every Thursday,' Chris answers.

'But he's not gay, is he?' I ask.

'Queer as a three-dollar bill,' Lenny says. 'He's an actor! What do you expect?'

What does that have to do with it, I want to know.

'All actors are gay,' Lenny replies matter-of-factly. 'Actually, that's not true, although a lot of people think they are. In reality, it's probably closer to 75 per cent.'

I find this statistic hard to believe and tell him so.

'Well, let me ask you this,' Karl says. 'What percentage of male hairdressers do you think are gay? And figure skaters, ballet dancers, interior decorators, flight attendants?'

'Don't forget librarians,' Lenny adds.

I think about it and concede that most of the men in these professions are probably gay, likely even more than 75 per cent. But acting isn't the same thing, I tell them.

'Honey, you are naive,' says Christopher. 'Acting is one of those trades where it just helps to be flamboyant, not to mention sensitive. Gay men are just drawn into it. Tell you what, go into any drama school in this country and talk to the boys. You'd be hard pressed to find a single straight male. And, what's more, it's obvious almost right away. Just about every student is a swishing queen.'

'Here's a good rule of thumb,' says Karl. 'Take the résumé of just about any movie star and look at where they started out. If they took drama in college, the odds are they're queer. If they started in theatre or did a stint on Broadway, especially musical theatre, bingo, they're gay. And I'm not talking 75 per cent, I'm talking 95 per cent.'

'Like who?' I ask somewhat sceptically.

Wrong question; or maybe the right one – it's like a verbal

stampede as all three of them start tossing out famous names, one after another, some of them A-list superstars. I'm not exaggerating if I say they went on for at least 15 minutes.

Then Karl finally puts a stop to it: 'You know, this might be faster if we just list the heterosexual stars.' Then they start tossing out those names, and indeed the list is noticeably shorter. 'Brad Pitt, Sylvester Stallone, Bruce Willis, Mel Gibson, Hugh Grant, Arnold Schwarzenegger, Colin Farrell . . .' At the next name offered by Christopher, he is stopped by Lenny.

'No, you can definitely cross him off the list. I know for a fact that he is fucking [well-known male Hollywood producer].'

I almost suspect that they are abusing my apparent naivety – or perhaps their list is merely wishful thinking – so I finally interrupt the litany. 'First of all,' I protest, 'half the people you mentioned are married.' This prompts shrieks of laughter from my new friends.

'He's a babe in the woods,' Karl says.

The three of them decide it's time to give me a tutorial on the way things work for a gay actor in Hollywood. 'Like we said,' Christopher recaps, 'drama schools are almost all populated by gay men. That much is easy to prove, because at that point in an actor's career there's no reason for him to hide it. In fact, at that stage, it's almost an advantage to be gay because a straight guy is in the minority. And, by the way, that's why the sexuality of most stars is such common knowledge. At some time they were openly hanging out in gay bars or cruising online, and their secret is common knowledge by a large segment of the gay community wherever they're from. By the time they head back into the closet after hitting it big in Hollywood, it's too late.'

He then asks me to list the male Hollywood stars that are out of the closet. I can list them on one hand, with fingers to spare.

'Now, how is it possible that thousands of drama students – the overwhelming majority, in fact – and most Broadway actors are demonstrably gay, yet virtually every movie star is a raging heterosexual? The answer is, it's not.'

They start with a history lesson. I think they will begin with the obvious – Rock Hudson – but instead they use the example of James Dean, the ultimate Hollywood male sex symbol of the '50s whom I didn't even know was gay. 'Not only was he gay,' explains Lenny, 'but his sexuality, which he supposedly didn't even bother to hide, was causing shit-fits at the studio. They'd had plenty of experience handling gay actors before, but here they had this incredibly bankable star, worth millions, and he was cavorting around town with every fag you could think of, including another one of their big stars, Montgomery Clift. They were terrified the news would get out and his box-office potential would go down the crapper. So they pretty well forced him to start dating starlets while their publicity department went to work portraying Dean as a great cocksman.'

'The stakes were huge,' he continues, 'and there was enormous pressure from the studio for Dean to get married. Their preference was Natalie Wood, who was perfectly willing to act as Dean's beard, but both Wood and Dean were apparently reluctant to go along with the phoney nuptials.'

It's here that I interject. Do they really think America was so homophobic that people would stop going to his movies just because they thought he was gay?

'Well, at that time, yes, definitely. But that wasn't the real point with Dean,' Lenny replies. 'The fact is that part of his huge box-office appeal was that American girls were so in love with him that they would go to his pictures over and over again. Ironically, gay men did the same thing, but that's just an interesting side fact.'

Lenny then named a superstar actor of today and drew a parallel to Dean. 'Look at [one of the top box-office stars in the world]. At the beginning of his career, he had a lot of quirky roles and was never really seen as a leading man, so he didn't really bother trying to hide his gayness. But all of a sudden he starred in [hugely popular film] and almost overnight became a sex-symbol superstar. The studio surveys showed that 14- and 15-year-old girls were going to the movie over and over again, some as many as 20 or 30 times. And why? Because they liked to fantasise that they were his leading lady and that he was seducing them. If they knew he was gay in real life, that was all threatened. So, the next thing you know, he's dating supermodels and going to strip joints, while his publicist makes sure the news is plastered in every newspaper in the world. Funny, you never heard of him having a girlfriend during the first ten years of his career.'

Christopher explains that it's not necessarily homophobia per se that keeps actors closeted today, rather this phenomenon of both men and women attending movies to fantasise about bedding the star. 'Look what happened to Anne Heche after she came out as Ellen Degeneres's girlfriend. She had already been signed to star opposite Harrison Ford as his love interest in *Six Days, Seven Nights*. When the film came out, it completely tanked. Not because it was terrible but because men could no longer go to her movies and picture themselves boffing her. And not long after that, look what happened. Heche broke up with Ellen and, surprise, she's straight again.'

Lenny interrupts him. 'Well, it's not entirely true that homophobia has nothing to do with it. Look at all the black fags who don't dare come out because the American black community is so homophobic.' He names a black comedian with a penchant for transvestites. 'He's not really a sex symbol, he's a comedian, so technically he could come out, but if he does, he can say goodbye to his black fan base forever. Kaput!'

At this stage, I point out that the star is married. I can understand why he got married, but what's in it for the woman, I ask?

'Ah, that's the sixty-four-thousand-dollar question,' says Lenny. 'We spend a lot of time debating that very point and nobody can agree on the answer. In some cases, we know for sure that the women do it for career reasons. They are basically promised that if they marry a particular superstar actor, they are guaranteed that their own acting career will take off and they will be offered juicy roles because their new husband has so much clout with the studios. That much makes sense. What we don't know is how many of these women are actually lesbians.'

He explains that while the overwhelming majority of male actors are gay, the same is not true for females. 'If 7–10 per cent of women in regular society are dykes,' he says, 'then that's probably the percentage in Hollywood as well. Now, we all know for sure who some of the famous dykes are. [He names a multiple Academy Award winner who lives openly with her long-time girlfriend, another well-known actress, but has never officially acknowledged her sexuality.]

'And then there's Rosie O'Donnell – a perfect example. When she started out, she was as far from a leading lady as you can get. She made absolutely no attempt to hide her sexuality. When she was starring in *Grease* on Broadway, she began a long relationship with one of her female co-stars. Then she's hired to front a popular daytime talk show, watched by a lot of conservative Midwest housewives who wouldn't be very keen on watching a dyke host. Suddenly, she starts talking about the crushes she has on various male actors. She constantly refers to one in particular as her "boyfriend". Then when her lesbian friends call her on this, she tells them she's obviously joking, especially because the star in question is widely rumoured to be gay. So the whole thing is an elaborate inside joke. Then within days of the show coming to an end, Rosie finally announces that she is a lesbian.'

Then there are the women who date or marry gay actors. 'The most famous Hollywood beard today,' says Lenny, 'is [well-known Oscar-nominated actress], who has been reported to be dating a number of different A-list actors over the years. Everybody in Hollywood knows she's a dyke. You can be sure that if you see an item in the gossip columns reporting that she's dating some actor, then that actor is a fag.' He shoots off the names of three famous actors, each of whom is reported to be a notorious womaniser. Sure enough, all three of them have 'dated' the actress in question within the last few years.

'But what's in it for her?' I ask.

'That's easy,' says Lenny. 'Just as the gay rumours get dispelled whenever these actors are reported to be dating a beautiful woman – or more often when they are photographed with her in public – she gets to look like a breeder whenever it's reported that she is dating this or that handsome actor. Meanwhile, she has been dating [another well-known Hollywood actress] for years with the public none the wiser. So, it's basically a win–win situation for a lesbian actress to date or marry a gay actor. But then there's another subject that we can never agree on: bisexuality.'

'There's no such thing!' yells out Karl.

'Oh, shut up,' Lenny replies. He explains that nobody really knows how many of these gay actors are simply dating and marrying beards, and how many of them are actually bisexual. This debate, he says, has been raging since the beginning of Hollywood.

He cites the example of Cary Grant, one of Hollywood's greatest sex symbols. Grant, he says, was reportedly in love with the movie star Randolph Scott. 'Literally *everybody* in Hollywood knew it. They would sit there in the Brown Derby till all hours, staring longingly into each other's eyes and holding hands. They even shared a beach house together. Yet Grant was married five times. His wives had to have known about him and Scott, not to mention his other lovers over the years. One book claimed that he even had an affair with Marlon Brando, another rumoured bisexual. So why would anybody marry him in the first place? Were they lured by the promise of the fabulous glamorous Hollywood lifestyle and the money, or by the potential impact on their own acting careers? After all, three of his wives were struggling actresses.'

I actually remembered an incident in the early '80s when Chevy Chase was being interviewed by Tom Snyder and he said of Grant, 'I understand he's a homo.' Grant sued him for slander and won. It raises the question, how the hell does anybody prove anybody's actually gay, short of catching them in bed with a man?

Karl mentions one of the world's most famous sitcom stars who is gay and married. 'They live in this huge mansion, but according to people who have been there, he and his wife occupy half the mansion each and they never have anything to do with each other. Very convenient but, again, why did she marry him? I hear that the way these things work is the woman agrees to put in a certain amount of time before filing for divorce. In exchange, she is guaranteed a platinum credit card for the whole marriage and a generous settlement after the divorce. Hell, I'd marry some rich dyke looking for a beard. She wouldn't have to ask me twice.

'Then there's [recently married superstar actor], who's a little too close to being outed publicly for his own comfort. The story goes that he actually interviewed a series of women and offered them a huge sum of money, not to mention prime roles, in exchange for staying married to him for a certain number of years.'

He continues, 'The saddest part of the Hollywood closet for the gay stars who aren't bisexual is that they live a life of perpetual sadness. They can never really have an open relationship, so they end up having sex only with high-priced Hollywood call boys for $2,000 a night.'

'Unless Scientology gets its hands on them,' Lenny says.

The mere mention of Scientology piques my interest. 'What do they have to do with anything?' I ask.

'Well, if you pay them enough money and you're gay, they promise to convert you,' Lenny explains. 'Or so I hear.'

This sounds implausible to me. I certainly hadn't heard anything like it at my recent seminar. But Lenny insists that it is true. As part of L. Ron Hubbard's bizarre ideology, he explains, homosexuality is an illness which can be cured. And the Church has supposedly devised just the formula. 'That is why so many closeted Hollywood stars are drawn to the Church,' he says.

Lenny takes me over to the computer, does a quick Google search and, sure enough, there is a plethora of material about this phenomenon. In Hubbard's book, *Dianetics*, he wrote that the 'sexual pervert', by which he meant anyone practising homosexuality, lesbianism or sexual sadism, for example, was actually 'ill'. In *The Science of Survival*, he writes that no social order will survive which does not 'remove these people from its midst'. In the same book, Hubbard claims to be able to cure people of the mental problems that cause homosexuality.

Of course, this was all written a long time ago, when even the psychiatric profession labelled homosexuality a disease. It didn't necessarily mean that the present-day Church still believed this mumbo-jumbo. And besides, Hubbard was best known for science fiction.

But then we come across details of a 1998 lawsuit filed in the US District Court by a former Scientologist named Michael Pattinson. He claimed he turned to the Church to 'cure' his homosexuality after it used Scientologist John Travolta to illustrate how the Church could turn gay people straight. No other evidence or source I came across confirmed this view of John Travolta's sexuality, or the purpose of his involvement in the Church of Scientology.

But according to Pattinson's lawyer, Graham Berry, 'Michael was in a Scientology centre in Clearwater, Florida, with Travolta, and they used him as an example of someone who could be cured of what they referred to as his "ruin". However, after 25 years and $500,000, Michael is still gay.' Scientology spokesman Brian Anderson called the lawsuit 'tabloid litigation' and said Berry was using Pattinson as a puppet to extort money from the Church.

Travolta's lawyer, Jay Lavely, told the *New York Daily News*, 'This looks like complete hogwash. Travolta is a happily married man, which proves he isn't gay.'

Eureka! A good old-fashioned celebrity bitch fight.

I had finally found the inspiration for my documentary which, until now, had been looking like a total dud. Instead of my original plan, I would pose as a gay actor trying to make it in Hollywood.

I leave the poker game that night with a new perspective and a new film.

3

★ Royal Redheads and Travolta Rumours ★

'There is nothing gay in this movie [*Hairspray*]. I'm not playing a gay man. Scientology is not homophobic in any way. In fact, it's one of the more tolerant faiths. Anyone's accepted'
— *Hairspray* star John Travolta

'John Travolta is, like, one of the most gay-friendly people I know. He doesn't bring religion or Scientology into the workplace. And everyone on our set was gay. The producers are gay, the writers are gay, the composer is gay, the director is gay, all of the choreography team is gay'
— *Hairspray* director Adam Shankman

As far as I know, I've never had a very gay sensitivity, at least as far as my narrow stereotypes defined the term. I don't particularly like Bette Midler. I'm not very neat. And I like to sleep with women. But I was determined not to let these tiny details stop me as I went about becoming gay for my new role. I had always heard right-wing homophobes talking nonsense about how gays had a secret agenda to convert heterosexuals to their lifestyle. If only it were true and I could find a gay Church to transform my sexuality, at least temporarily; what I considered would be like Scientology in reverse.

But alas, it looked like I was going to have to do the job myself. When I inform my publicist of my plan, she is all too glad to help out.

'The first thing we're going to have to do is gay you up,' she declares.

She takes me to Carlos, the gayest 'hairstylist to the stars' she knows, to change my look. After a few snips, and a little styling gel, I look like a new man, definitely more effete than before. I'd date me. But there is still something missing. Next we head to a vintage-clothing store on Hollywood Boulevard, where we ask the proprietor for advice. 'Something loud,' he advises. 'A little disco flashy. I have just the thing.' (YouTube)

He pulls out a lime-green, sequined polyester shirt and a gold bow tie. 'Voila!'

If this doesn't get the boys' hearts aflutter, nothing will. But the transformation is still not quite complete. I sense that I need a whole new persona to go along with my new look. Nothing so over the top that it arouses suspicion, but something flamboyant.

Then it hits me. His Highness! Like Hollywood, there is a long and noble tradition of gay royalty dating and marrying female beards for the sake of public propriety. My new moniker will be an act of solidarity with the poor princes.

I'd always had an incongruous fascination with the British Royals, who had provided me with an inspiration for one of my favourite stunts a decade earlier.

In the early '90s, I was living in Montreal when one of the British tabloids revealed that Princess Fergie had cheated on Prince Andrew – a revelation that later led the way to their estrangement and divorce. A light bulb went on in my head and I knew that this was the moment I had long been waiting for: the opportunity to hoax the British press. This was a favourite sport amongst a select group I had befriended while living in London years earlier. These jokesters competed with each other to see who could make up the most outlandish story and get it printed in the newspapers. I had always admired their craft and wished I could join their ranks. This seemed like a golden opportunity because I happened to have been living in England when the royal engagement was first announced and couldn't escape the daily media bombardment of every detail of Fergie's life and upbringing. I still remembered many of the details as if it were yesterday and knew that this would be prime fodder for the stunt I envisioned, which I intended to document for my favourite magazine, *Private Eye*.

I immediately called up my old friend and writing partner, Max Wallace, and enlisted him in my plan.

First, we chose our patsy: the tabloid the *Sunday Mirror*. Max placed a call and asked to speak to the paper's Royal correspondent. When the journalist came to the phone, Max told him he had a friend, a Montreal musician, who had had an affair with Sarah Ferguson during the period when she was engaged but not yet married to Prince Andrew. He took down some of the salient details but was noncommittal about the paper's interest. He told Max he'd get back to him. We still hadn't heard a word by the next day and were already preparing to call another newspaper and renew our efforts when Max received a phone call. The man on the line identified himself as Ian Markham-Smith, a journalist for the *Sunday Mirror*. He had just flown into Montreal's Dorval airport, as he understood that Max had a friend who had slept with Fergie. His paper was willing to put up a considerable sum of money for the story, he said, and would even be willing to pay Max a finder's fee, if he arranged it. Markham-Smith was actually somewhat notorious because he was the reporter who, years earlier, had sued Sean Penn for assaulting him during Penn's marriage to Madonna.

Markham-Smith asked for a hotel recommendation and requested they meet later that day to discuss the matter. Max agreed to meet that evening in the hotel bar. He then called me and we agreed that I would actually meet with Markham-Smith, posing as Max, but first we had to come up with a convincing story.

The story we concocted went like this: I had been at a well-known West End London bar called Magic Moment one afternoon in the summer of 1986 with my friend, having a drink during happy hour, when two women, a blonde and a brunette, sat at a table next to us. When the blonde got up to go to the bathroom, the brunette saw my saxophone case and asked me if I was a musician. We got talking and she suggested that we all go to dinner together at a Chinese restaurant in Soho. After dinner, she asked me if I wanted to go back with her to her hotel. We took a taxi to a posh West End hotel and when we got to her room, she took off a wig to reveal the by then famous red hair. 'Nobody's going to believe you if you tell,' she had supposedly declared. Then she had told me about all the pressure she was under since the engagement had been announced, how she was already having doubts, how the Queen disapproved of her, etc.

We rehearsed the story over and over until it was time to meet with Markham-Smith. When I arrived, I explained to Markham-Smith – who, it turned out, had flown in from Los Angeles, not London – that my 'friend' was nervous about going public because his father was a prominent politician. He told me his paper would be willing to pay £50,000 for the story if they were convinced it was genuine and that they would pay me an additional £5,000 if I could produce my friend. I told him I'd try. As we drank, Markham-Smith told me some hilarious stories about his old boss, the former *Mirror* publisher Robert Maxwell, whom he called 'a fat old cunt'. He told me that his colleagues staged a huge rollicking party after the bombastic Maxwell had died at sea a year earlier.

When we finally parted, I told him I would do my best to produce my friend. The next morning he called again. I told him my friend wanted to meet him for lunch at the Four Seasons Hotel. At the appointed time, I showed up and revealed that I was actually Ian, not Max. I proceeded to tell him the entire story we had concocted the day before. I laced the story with lots of convincing detail, including some obscure facts I remembered from the media feeding frenzy a few years earlier. For example, one particular detail had always struck me. When Fergie was a young girl, she had apparently had a black horse that she named 'Nigger'. I told Markham-Smith that when I had informed Fergie that I was a big fan of the famous black jazz musicians Louis Armstrong and Miles Davis, she had said how embarrassed she was that she had once given her horse that name.

I was sure an experienced journalist such as Markham Smith would see through the tissue of lies that I was feeding him, but when I finished the tale, he had only one question: 'Did you fuck her?' When I replied in the affirmative, he asked, with a big grin on his face, 'Was she good?' I told him she was a tiger in the sack.

He told me they'd pay me £100,000 to tell my story and come back to London with him to be photographed at some of the key locations. I told him I was tempted, but I was a little reluctant because of the media circus I knew would ensue. He told me to think it over and get back to him soon.

The next morning he called me for my answer. I told him I still hadn't decided, at which point he upped the offer to £150,000 and told me he could help get me a book deal as well. At that point, I desperately wished I really had slept with Fergie. I was no gentleman and would have had absolutely no compunction about being labelled a despicable cad if it meant earning that kind of money.

I told him I'd give him an answer as soon as I talked it over with my family and I'd call him at his hotel when I came to a decision. The next morning he telephoned me again. He was no longer very jovial. 'Look, you've led me on a fucking wild-goose chase for three days. I've booked a flight back to LA this afternoon and I need an answer now.' I then told him that I had decided not to go public because I didn't want to put my family through the ordeal. He muttered something about wasting his bloody time and hung up.

Two days later, to our surprise, Max received a phone call from a *Daily Mail* journalist who had flown in from London to pursue a story about somebody who had bedded Fergie while she was engaged. We couldn't figure out how the hell a rival paper had got the story, as well as Max's phone number, unless either Markham-Smith or a *Mirror* employee had leaked it to them. Max revealed that the *Sunday Mirror* had already offered £150,000 for the story. He immediately said the *Mail* could do better. Max told him he'd try and convince his friend.

Then, the very same day, Max gets a phone call from a *Sun* editor, who tells him, 'You have half the newspapers in England chasing to Montreal for this Fergie story. What's going on?' Totally bizarre, and much more successful in some ways than I had anticipated, but it seemed nobody was willing to print the story unless I went public, which, as far as playing a hoax on the media went, was still something of a failure.

Then we hit on the idea to phone the worst newspaper we could possibly find, the trashiest of all tabloids – a paper even less credible than the *News of the World* – the *Sunday Sport*, boasting 'more boobs per page than any other paper'. I still remembered one of their classic front-page headlines: 'Chevrolet found on the moon', featuring a photo of an old car on the moon's surface. Surely a newspaper this trashy would print the Fergie story, no questions asked.

But to my surprise, when Max called to offer them the story, they did indeed ask questions. They even wanted to know what address I had lived at when I had this alleged affair and, for the sake of authenticity, Max truthfully told them 39 Exmouth Market. Two days later, we still hadn't heard back from them, so Max called the editor and asked if they had made any decision.

'Look, mate. We think you've made this whole story up,' he declared.

Why did he think that? Max wanted to know.

It turned out that the paper's researchers had tracked down the former landlord of the Exmouth Market flat I had lived in at the time. He, in turn, supplied them with the name of the guy whose name was on the lease, a University of London law student named Nigel. When they tracked him down, the guy told the *Sport* that he remembered renting out a room to a Canadian journalist chap. From that, the paper concluded that the whole thing was probably bogus.

So, in the end, some of London's largest and most 'respectable' tabloids had bought the story hook, line and sinker, but it took one of the world's trashiest rags to figure out the whole thing was an elaborate hoax. It was a fascinating insight into the British tabloid media and my closest ever connection to 'royalty'.

But I digress.

With my new persona of His Highness established and the gayest look I could summon ready for a test run, it was almost time to infiltrate the allegedly homophobic world of Scientology to see if they could turn me straight again.

But first I needed to do some further homework about Scientology and gays, an issue the *LA Times* piece had failed to address.

Although there are literally thousands of anti-Scientology sites on the web, I didn't trust any of them to supply an objective view of the religion because most seemed to have an axe to grind. Instead, I turned to a 1991 cover story about the Church in *Time* magazine, one of the world's most respected and credible media outlets. Judging by the headline, however, it didn't appear to be all that objective: 'Scientology: The Thriving Cult of Greed and Power'.

The article, by award-winning journalist Richard Behar, makes no bones about its view of the Church, which Behar claims was founded by L. Ron Hubbard to 'clear' people of unhappiness. Behar explains that Scientology portrays itself as a religion but in reality is 'a hugely profitable global racket that survives by intimidating members and critics in a Mafia-like manner'.

'Prosecutions against Scientology,' he continues, 'seemed to be curbing its menace'. The article says that hundreds of adherents of the religion, many of whom had admitted they were mentally or physically abused, had quit the Church and criticised it. Some sued them and won; others settled for amounts in excess of half a million dollars.

The Church had variously been called 'schizophrenic and paranoid' and 'corrupt, sinister and dangerous' by the judges overseeing these cases. The article called Hubbard 'part storyteller, part flim-flam man'. One judge in a case in California in 1984 concluded that the Scientology founder was 'a pathological liar'.

But that really wasn't what interested me most. Instead, the passage that caught my eye involved that famous member of the Church: John Travolta.

The Church's former head of security, Richard Aznaran, told *Time* that a Scientology ringleader 'repeatedly joked to staffers about Travolta's allegedly promiscuous homosexual behaviour'. Travolta refused to comment and his lawyer called the questions raised 'bizarre'. In the following weeks, however, the article relates, Travolta coincidentally announced that he was getting married to a fellow Scientologist, actress Kelly Preston.

According to the article, 'high-level Scientology defectors claim that Travolta has long feared that if he defected, details of his sexual life would be made public'.

'He felt pretty intimidated about this getting out and told me so,' recalled William Franks, the Church's former chairman of the board. 'If you leave, they immediately start digging up everything.'

I had never even heard a hint that Travolta was gay, although everybody has heard the rumours about another Hollywood Scientologist actor. But not so long ago, the *National Enquirer* published a photo of Travolta kissing another man on the lips while he was coming down the gangplank of a private jet at an airport in Ontario while Travolta was in town filming *Hairspray*, in which ironically he plays a woman.

Travolta's lawyer, Martin Singer, was quick to respond to the media uproar that resulted from the seemingly damning *Enquirer* photo. 'As a manner of customary greeting and saying farewell, Mr Travolta kisses both women and men whom he considers to be extremely close friends,' said Singer. 'People who are close to Mr Travolta are aware of his customary, non-romantic gesture.'

I wasn't sure about the ethics of outing a gay actor, especially one whose livelihood depends on remaining in the closet. And besides, Travolta seems like a thoroughly decent guy, very progressive and an ardent opponent of George W. Bush. Not at all like another of his fellow celebrity Scientologists, a notorious whack job also long rumoured to be in the closet.

One of the questions I grappled with for my documentary and this book was should I reveal some of the names supplied to me by my Hollywood contacts – thus guaranteeing a bestseller – or should I respect their privacy? It would be quite another story if I was writing an exposé on Washington politicians – I would have been tempted to out one of the many closet Republicans who are willing to tie themselves to a party with a despicable record of homophobia and moral hypocrisy; in fact, I wouldn't even have hesitated. But then there's the question: would outing a closeted actor or sports figure actually do more good than harm? After all, these are people with a huge public following, considered heroes by millions. Wouldn't it be a huge boost for equality and justice to reveal their sexuality so that kids from the Bible Belt raised to believe that gays are morally depraved could see that somebody they admire and look up to is actually gay? With hundreds, probably thousands, of gay teenagers committing suicide every year because of the shame or vilification they fear in coming out, might it even save lives to out a respected public figure?

Even so, I just couldn't bring myself to play God with people's lives.

After reading the *Time* article, my next stop was to hook up with the well-known Scientology defector Michael Pattinson, he of the 1998 lawsuit against Scientology and many of its top officials and adherents, including Travolta.

When I talked to him, Pattinson, a British expatriate, was still bitter about his long ordeal. I met up with him at his studio in West Hollywood, from where he now worked as a well-established artist. He was anxious to talk about this painful period in his life and I got the sense that talking to me about it was actually somewhat cathartic. He told me that he first encountered Scientology in 1973 when he was living in Paris and his doctor recommended Hubbard's book *Dianetics*. 'I had a stomach ulcer and the doctor actually thought Scientology might help me,' he explained. 'So I went to one of their centres in Paris and . . . soon I was hooked.'

The appeal for him, he said, was something he read by Hubbard in which the Church's founder promised he could cure people of their homosexuality through a process called auditing.

'You have to understand that back then where I came from – England – being gay was still very taboo,' he said. 'It was probably like the American South is now. So, along comes this religion that can supposedly make me straight. Of course that appealed to me.'

He said he kept taking the courses, which required paying higher and higher fees, anticipating that if he reached a high enough level he would finally be offered the auditing process that Hubbard had said could cure homosexuality.

Pattinson gets emotional as he tells me that he knows first hand about Hubbard's homophobia because he was a long-time friend of Hubbard's son, Quentin, who was also gay. In 1976, at the age of 22, the founder's troubled son committed suicide in Las Vegas.

'Hubbard could never accept that his own son was gay,' recalls

Pattinson, who says he was devastated by Quentin's death. 'His premature death was, I believe, the result of Hubbard's homophobia and cruelty. I was with Quentin two or three days before he died. He was absolutely distraught and destroyed because his father had just [demoted] him back to the bottom ranks of Scientology because of some technical mistake . . . The degree of hate and viciousness that Hubbard showed towards his own son was just a symptom of his cruelty. He basically destroyed his own son.'

Meanwhile, Pattinson was increasingly anxious to turn straight, in part to rid himself of the kind of depression and guilt that had plagued Quentin all his life.

'Whenever I asked, they would tell me to be patient but that eventually I would be ready,' he said. 'The case supervisor is the one who decides these things, but he kept putting it off. Meanwhile, I was spending a fortune on these courses.'

Pattinson says he was well aware that the Church placed an extreme importance on the public image of their high-profile members.

'I was treated by the same handlers as Tom Cruise, Kirstie Alley, John Travolta and other celebrities within Scientology,' he explains, 'and I know that it is very important for public relations that within the [film] industry some people are seen to be straight while actually being gay, and trying to handle it through Scientology . . . All this, of course, would be in their preclear folders under an assumed name, a codename, because their names couldn't get out. All their innermost secrets are there . . . They may have a secret that is seen to be terrible within the industry, so they would probably be very inclined to go into an arranged marriage to hide this fact.'

Pattinson said that nobody ever explicitly used Travolta as an example of a gay adherent who had been cured of his homosexuality by Scientology but that people inside the Church would constantly refer to the movie star as one who had been cured.

'I joined pretty well the same time as he did, knew all the same people. In fact, I was considered a celebrity, I think, even before he was, and was even once on the cover of the Church's magazine, *Celebrity*. Everybody knew about him early on. It was pretty obvious. Travolta was a role model for the cure, especially after he got married. I thought, well, if he could get married, he must be cured, and I took even more courses and spent even more money, just waiting for the day when I would also be cured of what they called my "ruin". Well, that day never came and finally I'd had enough.'

Pattinson eventually dropped the suit after he ran out of money, claiming that the Church's deep pockets made it impossible to fight the case any longer. 'They spent more than $2.5 million fighting it and it was obvious they were going to keep fighting it till I couldn't afford to pursue it any longer,' he claims.

When I studied Pattinson's actual court filing, I discovered a number of very bizarre details, which is not terribly unusual when studying Scientology. Still, I couldn't figure out whether the anti-Scientologists were even bigger nut jobs than Hubbard and the Church officials they claimed were trying to take over the world.

In Pattinson's lawsuit, John Travolta is named as a defendant. I couldn't quite figure out what he was supposed to have done to earn Pattinson's wrath, but one even more confusing clue can be found in the court filing:

> Defendant Travolta has knowingly participated in the intentional violation of the Establishment Clause of the First Amendment to the United States Constitution, thus instigating the 'excessive entanglement of church and state'. Defendant Travolta has known of Scientology's 'gulags' and 'concentration camps', otherwise known as RPFs, through both personal observation and information received from a certain former Scientologist, but has deliberately chosen to turn a blind eye to their existence and to refrain from disclosing his knowledge to people such as Plaintiff who trusted and relied upon him as a

principal spokesperson on behalf of the Defendants. Indeed, when the movie *Saturday Night Fever* was first released, he knowingly arranged for a hard copy of the movie to be shown to members of the Sea Org sentenced to armed confinement in the RPF, or 'gulag' in Scientology's buildings in Hollywood, California. Defendant Travolta's public statements, 'handling' and subsequent marriage were material statements Plaintiff reasonably relied upon, as Commodore Hubbard intended when he taught Defendants how to 'use' celebrities, such as Defendant Travolta, for the recruitment, brainwashing and retention of the Plaintiff and others.

I was damned if I could figure out what all that meant, or if I wanted to be delving too deeply into anything associated with gulags and concentration camps. But I figured those terms were probably a little hyperbole used for dramatic effect. At least I hoped so.

With Pattinson's nightmare ordeal fresh in my mind, I decide it might be time to join Scientology and experience the religion for myself. But first I paid a visit to a veteran reporter for the *Hollywood Reporter* named Barbara Sternig who had written a lot about Scientology and celebrities over the years.

'I can only assume the idea is to get them while they're young,' she tells me. 'Get them before they're successful and there will be a loyalty base there that will stand you in good stead forever. If you get another Tom Cruise coming out of that, another Lisa Marie Presley coming out of that, you have your income guaranteed for the future; you have a generation of money. I'm sure it is based on money, though the Church would probably deny that.'

According to Sternig, Hollywood is terrified about the rise of Scientology, so much so that it has skewed the results of Oscar voting on more than one occasion.

'There's allegedly a good reason why neither Travolta nor Cruise have won an Oscar,' she reveals. 'For example, look at Cruise's performance in *Born on the Fourth of July*. It was brilliant, tailor-made for an Oscar, but he was shut out. Then he was also denied for both *Jerry Maguire* and *Magnolia*. And, of course, Travolta was the odds-on favourite for *Pulp Fiction* and he should have won, but again he was shut out. It's fairly obvious that the Hollywood establishment don't want to see a Scientologist win an Oscar for fear that it will just help them recruit more celebrities and everyday members. Can you imagine the speech that one of them might make to a billion viewers if they actually won?'

She points to Cruise's ex-wife, Nicole Kidman, as a perfect example of this phenomenon. 'If you remember back to Nicole's brilliant performance in *To Die For*. All the reviewers were predicting she was a shoo-in for an Academy Award. That, of course, was when she was still married to Cruise and she was a practising Scientologist. She wasn't even nominated. Then a few years ago, only *after* she divorced Cruise and renounced Scientology, she won her Oscar. That's probably not a coincidence.'

Or perhaps Hollywood types refuse to vote for Scientologists come Oscar time because half the eligible voters are gay. But what do I know?

I really had no idea what to expect when I set out to invade Scientology's castle headquarters on Hollywood Boulevard. From what I had been reading, most of the world's anti-cult organisations regarded the religion as a sinister cult. I had heard countless stories of journalists attempting to invade other religious cults, such as the Moonies, who operate under the guise of the Unification Church. These journalists, the story goes, were quite knowledgeable about the Church's practices before 'joining' and were certain that they could withstand the cult's sophisticated brainwashing methods, which include sleep and protein deprivation. But before they knew it, they had been brainwashed into joining the Church. I didn't really think Scientology employed those kinds of methods but I packed a case of protein bars before I journeyed in, just in case. I also insisted that Melanie accompany me for some extra protection. And I brought along Miles as well, though I was fairly sure he would be turned away when they saw his video camera.

On the day in question, the three of us sweep up the steps and through the entrance. The receptionist seems a little taken aback to see me in my garish green outfit and asks what she can do for us.

Melanie quickly introduces me as 'His Highness Halperin'. She explains that I'm thinking of joining Scientology and want to take their personality test. A Church official immediately approaches us and says, 'No cameras.' I tell her (truthfully) that my uncle invented the credit-card key and that he has long been fascinated by Scientology. As an actor, I explain, I am also quite interested because of the Church's track record in producing celebrities. At this point, I can almost see the dollar signs light up in her eyes, calculating just how many tens of millions my uncle must have made from such an invention. Melanie explains that we are documenting my quest to become an actor on video, at which point the official finally relents and agrees to let the camera in. She insists on processing my membership and overseeing my test personally.

We walk through what can only be described as a shrine to L. Ron Hubbard. His photo and writings are everywhere, and it reminds me of a trip I once took to Soviet Russia where Lenin was omnipresent. The only difference is that his social experiment eventually ended up in the crapper, while Hubbard's seems to be thriving.

She brings me over to the table and produces a written test. 'Read the front page,' she tells me, 'fill out the top, open the booklet and start answering the questions. The front page will explain how to answer. When you're done, you'll get a computerised graph showing the strong points, weak points and from a viewpoint of improving something about your life. It will give you a good bird's-eye view of what's going well and what can be improved.'

I sign my name His Highness Halperin and list my address as the Rabbinical College of Montreal, then start to fill out the lengthy test.

The questions themselves seem rather innocuous, asking me variously if I find it easy to relax, if I have any regrets about past misfortunes and if I have the stomach to kill an animal to put it out of pain. (YouTube) I decide to answer each question the opposite way to how I really feel, just to see what will happen in the results.

While I'm waiting for them, I ask my Scientology handler whether the Church can really help my acting career take off. 'Obviously I'm not at the level of Travolta or Cruise,' I tell her, 'but are there any classes for me to take to help me become a star?'

'Absolutely,' she replies. 'I mean, that's what we do. We have courses that people can take where they learn how to, on the one hand, handle certain things in life that are causing trouble. It could be marriage, money or any other problem you might be having.'

'And you'll be able to tell with this test?' I ask.

'Yeah, it's actually very accurate,' she asserts.

I proceed to tell her that I am actually having a big problem. I'm gay and I'm worried that it might hurt my acting career.

Melanie jumps in. 'He needs this because he's so hung up about being gay,' she tells the handler. 'It's affecting his overall confidence. As an actor, he needs confidence to make it.'

'Do you think it makes any sense?' I ask.

'Sure. Absolutely,' she responds.

'Well, that's why I'm here, because I think my homosexuality is ruining my career. Is there any way to get over that?'

'Possibly,' she replies matter-of-factly.

I ask her how.

'Through auditing,' she replies.

'What's auditing?' I ask.

'Auditing is spiritual counselling.' (YouTube)

Then the penny drops. She suggests that I'm now ready for the

'E-meter' test. I had come across this bizarre device during my research and was somewhat apprehensive. The E-meter, otherwise known as the electroencephaloneuromentimograph, was introduced by Hubbard in the 1950s as a supposedly simplified lie detector, designed to measure electrical changes in the skin while subjects discussed private and intimate moments from their past. Hubbard argued that unhappiness sprang from mental aberrations (or 'engrams') caused by early traumas. Counselling sessions with the E-meter, he claimed, could knock out the engrams, cure blindness and even improve a person's intelligence and appearance. The US Food and Drug Administration actually stepped in at one point and sued the Church because of its claims about the effectiveness of the device.

In his 1971 ruling on the matter, District Judge Gerhard Gesell called Scientology a 'pseudo-science that has been adopted and adapted for religious purposes' and made reference to Hubbard's 'quackery'. He declared:

> Hubbard and his fellow Scientologists developed the notion of using an E-meter to aid auditing. Substantial fees were charged for the meter. They repeatedly and explicitly represented that such auditing effectuated cures of many physical and mental illnesses. An individual processed with the aid of the E-meter was said to reach the intended goal of 'clear' and was led to believe there was reliable scientific proof that once cleared many, indeed most, illnesses would automatically be cured. Auditing was guaranteed to be successful. All this was and is false – in short, a fraud. Contrary to representations made, there is absolutely no scientific or medical basis in fact for the claimed cures attributed to E-meter auditing.

The judge ruled that the Church could no longer advertise its services as a scientific cure and put forward the requirement that

Scientology label the E-meters as ineffective in treating illnesses. He also dictated that the device could be used only in 'bona fide religious counselling'.

But even more controversially, the E-meter is often used for something Scientology allegedly calls the 'sexual and criminal security check'. Given to members at different phases of their Scientology career, they are asked to hold onto the E-meter while they are asked questions about past criminal acts, crimes against Scientology and sexual deeds or misdeeds. It is during this exercise, according to stories that have circulated for years from Scientology defectors, that the Church garners embarrassing and incriminating information that can be used against members if they try to leave the Church or reveal its secrets. The questions supposedly given to new members, known as preclears, delve into subjects including rape, abortion, bigamy, cannibalism, sodomy and pornography, not to mention questions such as 'have you ever practised sex with animals?'

According to *The Scientology Scandal*, there are also 25 questions specifically concerning the respondent's feelings about Scientology. Among these, 'Have you ever had any unkind thoughts about L. Ron Hubbard?' and 'Are you coming on this course with the intention of killing off your body, with the intention of spinning or going insane?'

Needless to say, I did not relish the idea of being hooked up to this device and possibly revealing my true intentions towards Scientology. But what was the worst that they could do to me at this point?

4

★ Hooked up to E ★

I'm not exactly sure what to expect as I'm hooked up to the E-meter, but it's definitely not anything as innocuous as the questions they ask me. My handler explains that if the needle on the device moves it shows stress points, and that if it moves far enough to the right it's a 'fail', which indicates just how much I need Scientology. Then she asks the first question.

'Is anything bothering you today?'

Other than the prospect of being discovered as an undercover journalist and sent for 're-education' by being forced to watch the John Travolta Scientology epic *Battlefield Earth* for hours with my eyeballs propped open, I don't have a care in the world. This becomes obvious when the needle on the E-meter fails to move. It just sits there, as if the machine is broken. The handler looks nervous as she waits and waits for something to happen, appearing to will the needle to go haywire. I suspect the lack of movement is unusual. We both just sit there, staring at the needle for what seems like three minutes, until finally it moves a teensy bit to the right.

'You see,' she practically shouts with glee, 'that demonstrates a problem.'

73

Then she asks the next question.

'Are you nervous about something coming up in your life?' (YouTube)

Again, we both wait as nothing happens. Again, she looks nervous, as if she is calculating how much money I won't be shelling out to them to fix my problems. Perhaps it is she who fears having to watch the Travolta film, supposedly based on one of Hubbard's novels and on most critics' lists as the worst movie ever made. Or perhaps there is an even worse punishment (though I couldn't imagine how that's possible); maybe some weird Hubbardian science-fiction torture meted out to Scientology tour guides who fail to meet their sucker quota.

Again, the needle just barely moves. Again, she appears gleeful, nodding her head in sympathy, as if she has just seen test results showing that I have terminal cancer.

Then she says, 'Think about something, anything in your life, and focus on it.'

My mother had died just a few weeks earlier so that's the obvious thing to focus on. And naturally, the needle jumps to the right, about an inch. This time the handler can barely contain her excitement; in fact, I think she may have had a tiny orgasm as she watched the needle jump.

I tell her I was focusing on my homosexuality and how much it was screwing up my acting career.

'We can definitely help you with that,' she declares. 'You need auditing.' This is the second time she has suggested auditing. I'm beginning to sense a theme here.

By this time, the results of my personality test have come back in the form of a computerised graph. Not surprisingly, considering that I answered most of the questions the opposite of how I really felt, they reveal that I have a few issues. She announces that I'm stressed, depressed, insecure, emotionally fragile and slightly unstable. 'As I expected,' she says, 'you are under severe emotional turmoil, but you do have potential. I think Scientology can definitely help you with that. We have courses that you will benefit from greatly. It will turn your life around.'

Remembering Michael Pattinson and how much money he had doled out over the years, I try to press her about how much the courses will cost and how long they usually take, but she's non-committal. I'm still waiting for her to ask me more questions – perhaps to determine whether I was telling the truth about my sexuality – but to my disappointment, and relief, she tells me the test is over.

I'm actually somewhat surprised after all I have read that they didn't probe into my sexuality or anything of a remotely personal nature while I was hooked up to the E-meter, but I suppose they save that for when you're already reeled in.

At least I assume so, before I return home and do a little further research.

The idea that Scientology could 'cure' homosexuality originated in a booklet published by the Hubbard Dianetic Research Foundation in 1951. Entitled *Dianetic Processing: A Brief Survey of Research Projects and Preliminary Results*, it presented the outcomes of psychometric tests conducted on 88 people undergoing Dianetics therapy. The book claimed these case histories proved that Dianetics had cured 'aberrations', including manic depression, asthma, arthritis, colitis and 'overt homosexuality'.

That same year, *Handbook for Preclears* was published, in which Hubbard set out a list of instructions for Dianeticists to 'cure' homosexuality. After claiming that the cause of homosexuality was a fixation on a dominant parent of the opposite sex, he advised the homosexual could be 'rehabilitated' by severing this fixation. And, of course, he had written *Science of Survival*, in which he called for drastic action to be taken against sexual perverts.

He wrote that such people should be 'taken from society as rapidly as possible and uniformly institutionalised'. Sex criminals and political subversives were the 'slime of society', he claimed.

It is pretty gruesome stuff, but I discover that Hubbard had actually issued an edict in 1967 altering his previous extreme positions. He explained that it had never been his intention to 'regulate' individuals' private lives, as this had not resulted in positive outcomes. 'All former rules, regulations and policies relating to the sexual activities of Scientologists are cancelled,' he announced.

Whether the edict was disingenuous is anybody's guess but, five years later, the Church published *How To Choose Your People*, a book by Scientologist Ruth Minshull, which was copyrighted to Hubbard and given 'issue authority' by the Scientology hierarchy, meaning it had all the weight and credibility of a papal edict. Scientology churches were selling the book alongside Hubbard's own works until 1983. In the book, Minshull described the 'the gentle-mannered homosexual' as a classic example of a 'subversive' personality. She claimed gays to be 'social misfits' and wrote that it was not possible for them to feel love; their relationships were just 'brief, sordid and impractical meetings'.

It has actually long been rumoured that the homophobic writings of Hubbard might have come from his own embarrassment over his son Quentin's homosexuality.

A few years ago, a Scientologist wrote a pamphlet entitled *Straight Dope: About Gays and Scientology*. The pamphlet claimed that Hubbard had abandoned any earlier homophobia and that the Church's dedication to human rights and clinics designed to fight drug and alcohol addiction should be supported by the gay, lesbian, bisexual and transgender communities. The pamphlet said that it was through 'hate groups' spreading lies that the Church had been seen as a homophobic cult.

To illustrate the Church's changed views, in 2005 an article in *Source*, an official magazine published by the Church of Scientology, featured a story about a gay man and his partner.

Was all this merely window dressing to disguise what really went on behind the scenes with the Church and gays? I still had no idea. I suppose that I could have taken a bunch of courses and eventually determined for myself whether they were trying to convert me, but I hadn't the time, the money or the necessary dedication to my craft for the task.

What I did conclude is that the Church of Scientology is no more homophobic than fundamentalist Christianity or Orthodox Judaism, both of which still regard homosexuality as an aberration. In fact, Scientology seems to me officially more progressive on the subject, at least since 1967.

And even if the Church is trying to convert gays, I don't find that anywhere near as troubling as I do the Dalai Lama's staggeringly hypocritical public declaration that homosexuality constitutes 'sexual misconduct'. I expect this kind of bigoted clap-trap from a Catholic priest, not from somebody whose religion is dedicated to ending suffering and conflict. This is the man that millions consider to have attained enlightenment. If that's enlightenment, I'd rather remain ignorant. And don't even get me started on how women are treated in Tibetan monasteries. How can anybody worship such an anachronistic relic, whose followers often strike me as more cult-like in their devotion than even the Scientologists I encountered?

And what about the many American fundamentalist Christian denominations that sponsor what they call 'reparative' or 'conversion' therapy designed to change the sexual orientation of gay men and women. I recently read about one such programme, based in Memphis, Tennessee, called The Refuge, a youth programme run by an organisation called Love in Action International, which freely admits that this is their goal. It's actually run by a 'former' homosexual, who says he wants to put a 'guardrail' on the sexual impulses of young gays and lesbians. 'I've been out of homosexuality for 20 years,' he told a reporter, 'and for me it's a non-issue.' There are apparently more than 100 such programmes throughout the United States. So why is Scientology singled out?

In fact, as distasteful as Scientology and its tactics are to me, I honestly can't demonise the Church as I intended to do when I started my investigation. I found no real evidence that it is the sinister cult it's rumoured to be. Its most famous members are reasonably progressive politically and are not using the Church for right-wing moralising the way many other Churches do. Its campaign against psychiatric drugs, and psychiatry in general (which it calls 'Nazi science'), though extreme, makes many good points and appears to be validated practically every other week when a new study makes the headlines linking adolescent suicides to antidepressants, something Scientology has maintained for years.

And I came away honestly convinced that the Church's most successful members can attribute part of their success to the teachings of Scientology. Even Michael Pattinson acknowledged to me that his successful career as an artist can be partially attributed to his years inside the Church.

Of course, it's entirely possible that I was brainwashed during my sessions, that I was programmed to defend Scientology while hooked up to the E-meter and that my conclusions about the innocuousness of the Church are completely full of crap. So perhaps it's best to take them with a grain of salt.

5

★ Singin' in the Rain ★

Considerably more knowledgeable about the world of Scientology but still no closer to my real goal, I'm sitting in a Starbucks one day, dressed as His Highness, reading the trades, when a rather exotic woman sits down at my table. She says she loves my clothes and then asks me if I'm looking for a job.

'It depends,' I tell her. 'What did you have in mind?'

She introduces herself as Renata and describes herself as an 'entrepreneur'. I have no idea what that means until she says she might like me to join her 'stable'.

It takes me a little while longer to figure out that she runs an escort agency and that she's a madam. I tell her I may be interested, though I'm still figuring out if she wants me to work as a gay escort or as a gigolo.

'Tell me more,' I say.

She explains that she was the second-ever female to run her own 'service' in Hollywood after Heidi Fleiss, though technically speaking she operated out of Brentwood, not Hollywood. She started out running a brothel for the Russian mob, which she tells me was quite a lucrative career. Her mentor was an older mob-backed madam who taught her the ropes. But the venture came to an untimely end one day when the agency was raided by the police.

'They really came down hard on us, used helicopters and everything. I managed to escape without getting arrested, but that was the end of that agency, so I decided to start my own.'

Even if I'd not been doing a documentary about Hollywood, I would still have asked my next question.

'Do you get any celebrities?'

She is all too glad to oblige me with the gossip, perhaps thinking that it will tempt me to join her enterprise.

'We never got as many Hollywood celebrities as Heidi did in her heyday, but some days you would have thought our client list was the invite list for the Academy Awards ceremony.'

She is eager to name names as well as their sexual proclivities, and the first one she cites definitely surprises me – an Oscar-winning actor, who is considered one of the greatest superstars in Hollywood history.

'He liked to be pissed on, shitted on, the whole works,' she reveals. 'A male always serviced him, but I don't think he's queer, he's just adventurous.'

Her explanation just doesn't make sense to me, even though the actor in question is known as one of Hollywood's greatest womanisers.

'You see, you have to understand the life of somebody like that,' Renata explains. 'He's spent the last 40 years being worshipped and adored wherever he goes. People like that have so much money and so many things, they're not necessarily closeted but they want a new adventure.' Though she hastens to add that's not to say the majority of male actors who hire the gay male escorts are straight. Far from it.

'I've got two gay escorts working for me at the moment, one black, one Italian. They work every single day and one out of five of their calls is from a celeb.'

She proceeds to name about 15 regular famous clients who each request the male escorts. Most of the names surprise me, even after my shocking tutorial by the Queers of the Round Table.

'The funny thing is that celebs don't want to hire pretty girls or pretty boys; they can get that anytime,' she says. 'They just want somebody who's willing to fuck them with a dildo.'

A lot of very straight-laced actors, she says, want the black guy.

'They always say, for some reason, "I don't want him to touch me, I just want to touch him." And speaking of black guys, one of our best clients is [famous actor], who again I don't think is actually queer, but he obviously likes to dabble. That actually surprised me. I would have taken him for 100 per cent straight, although [another famous actor/comedian] is a fucking queer and everybody knows it. His preference is trannies.'

She tells me the going rate for everyday clients is $300 per hour, $500 if they want something 'freaky'. But celebrities and other prominent Hollywood clients are charged much more. She names a famous boxer who pays $5,000 to 'get bruised while getting shagged' by a female.

'Often the celebrities will hire one of our boys or girls to accompany them on a trip for a week. For that, they pay a minimum of $4,000 a day, sometimes much more. And sometimes there's no actual sex involved; they just want a woman travelling with them so they can get their picture taken with a female.'

She tells me about one of her clients, a very high-ranking executive at Universal Studios whom she describes as a 'divorced closet queer', who hires a female escort, asks her to bring a guy along and 'gives us autographs from celebrities as a tip'.

She then names a slew of famous rappers, each one a client. 'The funny thing is that many of them were pimps themselves before they became famous.'

I ask her how easy it is to recruit talent.

'Not hard at all,' she says. 'It's Los Angeles. Every girl I hire has a dream of being a movie star. It all goes back to the '70s when [famous Oscar-winning actress] worked as an escort for Platinum. She used that to become a model and eventually an actress. That's why most of our girls do it. They figure if it worked for her, it'll work for them. Of course, I've never seen a single other girl in this business get movie work.'

To my amazement, she tells me that her agency has more than one Catholic priest as a client and all of them request the boys.

'And on top of the priests, we have too many rabbis and ministers to count. I think our employees help them find God.'

She says she has so many police officers as clients that she feels relatively safe, though that didn't help her first agency avoid a raid. She also has at least one judge and one district attorney as regular clients.

'In this business, you can't operate too long in one place. It's not really ever safe, to tell you the truth. Heidi was stupid. She was too obvious about what she was doing. It was inevitable that she would get caught. I'm thinking of setting up shop in Manhattan in a couple of years, which is a licence to print money, and actually a safer place to operate from. Because so many politicians there use escorts, they never crack down.'

I'm still unclear about why a movie or rock star would need to pay for sex, though.

'The same reason why most people hire a pro,' she explains. 'A hooker doesn't judge you. Their job is to listen and to do whatever you pay them for.'

She gives some examples of what the various celebrities like to do, to illustrate why they turn to a prostitute instead of their partner.

'[A-list male actor and Academy Award nominee] loves to be handcuffed, tied up and gagged. [Famous television star] likes to choke a girl while his friend watches. [B-list movie star] wants a girl to shit on him and then he eats it. Well, maybe not, but he supposedly rubs it all over his face.'

She sees the look of disgust on my face.

'I'm serious,' she says. 'You wouldn't believe the kinds of things some people request.'

She says that while many celebs are 'total pricks', the three nicest are [a famous actor who specialises in Mafia roles; a former world middleweight boxing champion; and the aforementioned superstar male actor and Oscar winner].

'They're total gentlemen, which is why I was a little surprised when I learned about what perverts they are in bed.'

She reveals that [famous male movie star turned director] once gave one of her girls a $12,000 tip.

'How much do you think I can make if I work for you?' I ask.

'It depends on what you're willing to do,' she replies. 'You could make as much as $10,000 a week, but probably closer to $5,000, or a little less, to start out. And if you don't do drugs, you could save enough to buy a place in Malibu.'

She tells me that her hookers can decide for themselves what they are or aren't willing to do sexually, and that they're required to lay down the boundaries for the client before settling on a price.

'The sicker or kinkier the act, the more you can charge,' she explains. 'But the safety of my girls and boys is paramount. That's why we've installed hidden video cameras, though the clients don't know it. And we never watch them unless there's a problem. They get erased immediately after. For some of these guys, the only way they can get hard is to beat a girl up, though most treat their escorts better than their mistresses.'

I ask her if she's ever worked as a hooker herself.

'I did it a long time ago, but I hated it. Eventually, I turned gay. It really fucks with your head, but the money's so good, you don't want to give it up.'

It wasn't the best sales pitch, but I had to at least give her marks for honesty. And the money was indeed tempting. Moreover, what better way to get the inside scoop on Hollywood celebrities than to actually get inside a Hollywood celebrity? Unfortunately, there was only so far I was willing to go for my craft and I tell her thanks, but no thanks.

So far during my stay in Hollywood and my numerous interviews with young actors, I sensed a genuine desperation on the part of these young people to succeed in the movie business. It was really quite sad, and I was growing more sympathetic towards them every day. I decided to try a little social experiment to determine just how desperate they really were.

I took my royal court to the café at the Best Western Hollywood Hills Hotel on Franklin Avenue, a place where young actors hang out, practising their lines and trying to schmooze their way to the top. I brought along my buddy, Kris Kostov, who was in town trying to pitch his music to major labels. He had volunteered to be my court jester for the occasion. I wore my His Highness outfit and sat going through a huge stack of paper that I'd made look like a movie script. Kris's assignment was to spread the word that His Highness, a member of a royal family and a film producer, was in town casting for his new feature film.

Within minutes, someone took the bait. The first person to approach was Jessica, a 19-year-old actress from the Midwest. She asked me about my project and I explained it was going to be a major biopic based on the life of Cirque du Soleil founder Guy Laliberté.

Like me, Laliberté is from Montreal. Unlike me, he is a billionaire and one of the world's most successful show-business moguls, having taken a small street-busking troupe of acrobats and turned it into an internationally renowned entertainment act. I was good friends with Guy's former common-law wife, Rizia, and she had indeed told me enough stories about her ex to make a blockbuster film. But, for now, the project would have to be a mere foil for the antics of His Highness.

Once I mentioned Cirque du Soleil, Jessica immediately wanted in. She had seen a performance in Las Vegas and told me it was the most entertaining show she had ever seen. I told her she would be perfect for the part of Guy's daughter but that she should know up front that I didn't intend to pay any of the actors. Instead I had come up with a scheme that was going to change Hollywood forever – profit sharing.

The way it worked, I explained, was that the actors themselves invest in the film because they believe in it and in return receive a generous piece of the backend.

'This way we aren't beholden to the big studios and we don't need to compromise the artistic integrity of the film to satisfy the whim of some soulless studio executive,' I say.

She ate it up. Right then and there, she took out her mobile phone and called her father, a successful surgeon. After she explained the concept to her dad, she asked for a bank transit number so he could wire me $30,000.

This I wasn't expecting. I was beginning to realise that these people were not only desperate to make it in showbiz but were also extremely gullible. I had an uncomfortable vision of FBI agents storming in and placing me under arrest for interstate fraud. Of course, I also had a vision of myself driving out of the car lot that afternoon in a new Porsche.

'We're getting a little ahead of ourselves,' I tell her. 'I need to consult with my partners before I offer anybody the part.'

Fifteen minutes later, I'm drinking green apple Martinis with an actor named Greg.

'Cirque du Soleil,' he says. 'I want to play Guy. I'll shave my head, get a tattoo on my back . . . do anything to get the part.'

When I tell him about the investment, he says he can probably get a bank loan for about $10,000 to be part of this.

I tell him he might be a little young to play Laliberté but that he should send me a head-shot and I will arrange for a screen test in the near future.

Over the next three hours, I give the same spiel to seven different actors. Only two balk at investing their own money in my project. In fact, I 'raise' about $85,000 in financing for the film by the time I shut down the operation.

An unscrupulous producer could clean up in this town, preying on the vulnerability of these desperate kids. Damn my mother for instilling actual values in me!

I also see a different kind of desperation. While hanging out with Dan Di Julio, I had got to know one of his friends, a young actor named Daniela Pinto, a voluptuous blonde from Orange County. Pinto seemed very well connected and she took me to a number of parties. In fact, at one of these parties – a cocktail reception held by a Rodeo Drive fashion house – I met the '50s starlet Debbie Reynolds, who had starred in my mother's favourite movie, *Singin' in the Rain*. Reynolds, a very sweet old lady with an encyclopedic knowledge of Hollywood history, told me something that would have come as a surprise a few months earlier but no longer seemed a big deal.

'Every man I ever dated in Hollywood turned out to be gay,' she revealed. She had actually famously been married to Eddie Fisher – father of her daughter Carrie, aka Princess Leia – whom her old friend Elizabeth Taylor stole away from her, causing one of Hollywood's all-time-greatest scandals. I didn't have the guts to ask her if that applied to Fisher as well.

Reynolds was looking good for her age. She must have been in her early 70s and I almost expected her to get up and dance her way across the room like she did in the movie. Of course Gene Kelly and Donald O'Connor weren't there to sweep her off her feet and when I lamented the fact, she told me something that surprised me.

'Before that picture, I had never danced before. Never. But Gene could have taught an amputee to tap.'

The fact that Reynolds looked so young was hardly surprising. Botox, like silicone, runs like water in these parts.

There were probably other celebrities at the party, but I didn't recognise anybody else. And besides, meeting Reynolds was good enough for one evening. She was a dame that just oozed the glamour of old Hollywood, classy right down to her elegant Chanel suit, which was a refreshing change from the phoneyness that I had encountered since I first set foot in Tinseltown.

Reynolds reminded me of my old British landlady, Betty Hawkins, who told me she had taken care of Judy Garland during the last years of her tragic life when she lived in London. Hawkins – who had also cooked for a time for both the Queen Mother, whom she described as 'a drunken old tart, pissed as a newt and pickled in gin', and Princess Anne, who she described as a 'royal tightwad' – told me that every single one of Garland's five husbands was gay. 'Some women just don't like sex, but they do enjoy hanging around witty gay men who they can shop and gossip with.'

But I digress.

Everyone liked Daniela – except for the casting agents, who prefer slender, younger actors with a lot less education. Daniela was 31, weighed 154 lb and had an MBA.

'After I completed my MBA, I decided I wanted to pursue my real passion – acting,' she told me. 'Unfortunately, in this town you have to look as if you haven't eaten a meal in weeks. And if you have a brain, they don't want to know because then they can't fuck you over.'

One night, I was scheduled to accompany Daniela to the premiere of a new Pierce Brosnan film. She knew one of the organisers of the event and had managed to get a couple of passes. When I arrived at Daniela's West Hollywood apartment to pick her up, there was no answer. I waited more than half an hour, then headed back to my hotel disappointed. Two hours later, I received a call from her roommate, who had arrived home that afternoon to find Daniela sprawled on the floor, semi-conscious, with a bottle of pills and a suicide note. She had called an ambulance, which took Daniela to the hospital in time to have her stomach pumped.

Her roommate refused to show me the note, but I spoke to Daniela when she was released a day later after agreeing to become a psychiatric outpatient, and she explained what had happened.

'I went to a casting call yesterday afternoon and the agent told me she loved my acting. But she didn't give me the part because she said I was too fat. She didn't even use a euphemism. She just came right out and told me I was fat, as if I'd appreciate her honesty or something. Same story I keep getting from every fucking casting agent in this town, though usually they just say I don't "fit the description" of the character I'm reading for. I'm just so fed up with all this shit; it's driving me over the edge. When I got home, I just felt like dying – and on a whim I decided to do it instead of talking about it.'

I used to run a yoga retreat in the Laurentians and I convinced Daniela to go for spiritual healing at one in Hermosa Beach where they emphasise mind and body healing. After two weeks, she told me she felt like a new person. And even though she's now lost almost 25 lb, her acting career hasn't progressed at all, not for a lack of talent but because she still hasn't recovered the confidence that was sapped out of her over the years and that one needs in abundance to make it in this town.

6

★ Almost Famous ★

It was fun hanging out with the hookers and the religious whack jobs, but I still had a documentary to produce and I was failing miserably. If I didn't get results soon, I was afraid the network would fire my ass.

'It's time for you to do your job,' I tell my publicist, Melanie. 'When the hell are you going to get me some auditions?'

'Well, frankly,' she says, 'you still don't have the look of an actor.' She then tells me I need to lose 15 lb. 'You're looking a little porky. You need to go on a macrobiotic diet.'

It doesn't sound terribly appetising, but I suppose if I'm going to be an actor, I should starve myself in the Hollywood tradition of the skeletal starlets who live on carrots and air. As objectionable as this idea is, especially given the plight of my friend Daniela, I'm beginning to realise that this is the sick Hollywood reality. Still, it's nowhere near as bad for a man as it is for the women who are almost literally expected to starve themselves for a role. Melanie's friend Elissa Gross has cooked for such stars as Madonna, David Duchovny and Brad Pitt, and she was currently the personal chef of Anthony Kiedis, lead singer for the Red Hot Chili Peppers. She had agreed to have me over for a meal to see how I liked it.

The first thing I did was find Dan Di Julio, the Canadian actor whom I had followed at the beginning of my film and who was now even closer to being homeless. I figured he could use a good free meal.

When we arrive at her place, we sit down and she immediately starts bringing us salads, asparagus, spreads and healthy breads. To our surprise, it's actually delicious. At one point, when she goes into the kitchen to retrieve the next dish, Di Julio actually shoves some asparagus in his pocket to take home. Poor sod.

'I'll give you a basic diet,' she tells me, 'and you'll lose 15 lb in no time, but the real secret is to completely eliminate sugar. That stuff is pure evil. The Red Hot Chili Peppers don't eat anything with sugar and since they cut it out, their energy levels have doubled. It's very noticeable now when you watch them in concert. Even the rock critics have noted the change.'

Of course, I care less about her diet tips than I do about her dishing the dirt on Madonna.

'She's very nice, but very cheap. She watches every nickel she spends,' Elissa tells me. 'Even though she has, like, a billion dollars, it's impossible to pry money out of her without a struggle. She's a very sharp businessperson. People think she's turned Jewish just for the Kabbalah, but I think she's Jewish because she's so cheap,' she jokes. Of course, since Elissa and I are both Jewish, I refrain from calling the Jewish Defense League to have her legs broken for that remark.

Next up in Melanie's plan to make me into a movie star is some conditioning to tone me up. She knows just the guy to get me buff: Cliff Boyce, personal trainer for R&B superstar Usher. Unfortunately when she tries to contact him, she discovers that Boyce is busy on the set of Usher's new music video, being shot that week in LA. However, when she tells me the news, I'm undaunted.

'I'll go see him on set,' I tell her.

'Are you crazy?' she replies. 'They'll never let you anywhere near Usher.'

'Not only will I get on set,' I assure her cockily, 'I will get myself a part in the video. Just watch.'

The next morning, I head over to the lot in North Hollywood where the video is shooting. I'm expecting a couple of trailers, but when I arrive, I find sixteen trailers and seven massive trucks of equipment. It looks like they're shooting a full-scale Hollywood epic.

I approach the security guard at the barricades and tell him I'm there for the video. 'My name's His Highness Halperin,' I announce.

He looks me up and down and says, 'You look like a gay leprechaun.'

'That's who I play in the video,' I tell him.

He laughs and waves me through without even checking my name on his list. I suppose it doesn't hurt that I'm accompanied by Miles.

One of the first people I encounter on set is Usher's personal hairstylist, Stacy Gray. I tell her that I'm here to audition for a role in the video.

'Do you think I have a shot?' I ask.

'Absolutely not,' she replies. 'Not one shred of anything in me thinks that you can be cast in this video now.' (YouTube)

'Why not?'

'Because we're making history right now. We're doing 2005 *Thriller* and you're looking more like 1988 Urkel [the geeky character from *Family Matters*].'

'So, you think I should change the look?' I ask her.

'Absolutely. It's imperative you change the look.'

She points me to a trailer where she says I can find Cliff Boyce. Inside, there is a treadmill, free weights and two exercise bikes. I introduce myself and mention Melanie's name. Then I ask Cliff if he thinks I have a chance of getting a role in the video.

'Sure, because you're looking gangster,' he says.

I can't tell if he's humouring me.

'You really think I can make it?'

'Sure,' he replies. 'The fact that you came with the shades on . . . it's a wrap. All you have to do now is step in the spotlight.' (YouTube)

I tell him that I actually came by because Melanie thinks I have to get in shape before I can start landing roles.

'Get on that bike,' he tells me. 'I'll give you a workout.'

About ten minutes of furious pedalling later, Usher comes in and steps on the treadmill. He tells me he digs my outfit. 'I need to get me one of them gold bow ties,' he says with a grin. We start talking about music, mostly trivia about Miles Davis and his downfall. He seems impressed by the depth of my musical knowledge.

When I tell him I play the sax, he says, 'Ah, the devil's horn! Maybe I'll get to hear you blow sometime.'

I tell him I'm here to land a part in his video, but he tells me there's nothing available for a 'white boy'. 'Brothers only this time around,' he says apologetically.

I meet up with Melanie later. 'OK,' I tell her, 'I'm getting in good shape now. It's time to get me a gig.'

'You may be in shape physically,' she counters, 'but not yet mentally.'

I have no idea what the hell she's talking about, but the following evening she takes me to the launch of some flaky New Age book where she says I will probably encounter some celebrities.

'You need to get some spiritual enlightenment,' she tells me.

Sure enough, when we get to the launch, the place is teeming with D-list celebrities.

Melanie pulls me over and introduces me to Marla Maples, the ex-wife of the billionaire developer Donald Trump.

'The reason I moved from New York to LA,' she tells me, 'is

because I felt more spiritually connected here. I felt it was easier to stay in touch with my spiritual side here.'

'Where do you think you would be without spirituality?' I ask her.

'Oh God, I don't even want to think about it. I think the saddest thing of all is to be born without the desire to know God.'

Melanie suddenly tugs on my arm and pulls me over to meet Melissa Rivers, who has become somewhat well known for accosting celebrities with her mother Joan on the Academy Awards red carpet and commenting on their fashion choices. It seems that Melissa too can't help but share her spiritual enlightenment with anyone who will listen.

'I end every night by . . . call it meditation, call it praying, call it whatever you want. It's the only way to keep real in this town. You know, LA is a big, giant company town and people in the arts, I think, are more in touch with their spirituality.' (YouTube)

The *pièce de résistance*, however, is my encounter with the Hollywood guru Deepak Chopra, who brags about his stable of celebrity clients, including Demi Moore, Madonna, Michael Jackson and Oprah Winfrey. When I ask him how I should go about making it in Hollywood, he counsels me to 'live your life from the level of your soul'. Only then, he advises, will I find true success.

The more I listen to this gibberish, the more sensible Scientology starts to sound. At least they produced superstars John Travolta and Tom Cruise, not to mention rock and roll princess Lisa Marie Presley. Meanwhile, this flaky New Age mumbo-jumbo appears to have turned out a slew of washed-up has-beens. I think if it was up to me, I'd much rather star in a flick like *Pulp Fiction* than end up married to a rich blowhard with a bad comb-over, even if it meant being brainwashed, having my balls hooked up to electrodes and worshipping at the altar of a crazy old science-fiction coot. But that's just me.

When I tell Melanie that I can't take any more of this nonsense, she tells me the best is yet to come. 'Just wait till you see what I have in store for you tomorrow,' she promises.

As we're walking back to the car, we pass a huge wall mural featuring a number of Hollywood legends – James Dean, Marilyn Monroe, Humphrey Bogart . . .

Pointing, Melanie shouts, 'Look, there's Marilyn Monroe. Who does she want to be sitting next to? His Highness. There's a space for you right here! Do you want to be there? You will, you will. See this space here [pointing to a gap in the mural between Marilyn and Humphrey], it's like they left this space for you.' (YouTube)

I would probably have been thinking the woman had lost her mind if I hadn't been too busy asking myself how in God's name I chose her as my publicist.

The next afternoon, Melanie picks me up and takes me to a rather run-down neighbourhood. We pull up in front of a sign advertising 'Madame Sonya. Psychic readings'.

'You've got to be shitting me,' I say.

'You won't be disappointed,' she assures me.

We're greeted at the door by Madame Sonya herself. 'Do you want to take off your glasses?' she asks me.

'Why?'

'I need to look into your eyes.'

I decide to play along. 'Have you ever predicted somebody would become famous and they became famous?' I ask her, as she looks into my eyes and takes my hand.

'Yes, we're very accurate.'

'So, if you predict I'm going to be famous, do you think eventually I have a chance to be?'

'You are going to be,' she declares. 'It's not eventually, you are. It's guaranteed you're going to be famous. I looked in your eyes and into your palms; it shows. That's why I needed you to take off the glasses.' (YouTube)

'Anything about the look?' I ask her. 'Should I keep the look?'

She looks me over and thinks about it. 'In my opinion, change the look. I really don't like that shirt and tie.'

I decide Melanie has wasted enough of my time. That evening, I call and ask her to meet me on Hollywood Boulevard at Kevin Spacey's star. When she arrives, it would be an understatement to say that she was perturbed at the sight that greets her. I am standing there wearing a sandwich board, which reads: 'His Highness Hollywood: Cast Me, I'm a Royal'. (YouTube)

She storms up to me screaming furiously. 'Are you kidding me right now? What are you doing? What the hell are you doing right now?'

'I'm trying to get cast on Hollywood Boulevard,' I tell her calmly. 'It's more than you've done for me. You've been on the job for days and I haven't even got an audition yet.'

'What the hell is standing on Kevin Spacey's star going to do for you? Are you kidding?' she bellows. By this time, we're drawing a crowd. 'You're embarrassing me. I have a reputation. I'll be a laughing stock.' Then she turns around, storms off and disappears into the night.

The next morning, Melanie knocks on the door of my hotel room. 'I'm going to take you today to teach you a lesson. I'm going to show you what happens if you don't listen to me.'

We're driving in her car and, obviously still pissed off because of last night, she says, 'I'm going to take you to meet Nikita Lea. Guess what she does. She's nude on the Internet.'

When we get to her place, Nikita is expecting us. It seems that she arrived in Los Angeles a few years ago with big dreams but turned to Internet porn when things didn't work out the way she expected. I suspect that Melanie thinks Nikita's career is going to serve as some kind of cautionary tale for me, but I've seen it all before.

Unlike the others I encounter, however, who have been lured into porn, Nikita hasn't given up hope of achieving her big break. She still goes out for auditions every day during pilot season and has landed a number of cable movies.

'I've had quite a lot of roles that you could call soft-core porn,' she reveals. 'Basically, I have to take my shirt off five times, which I don't mind at all. When I go out for mainstream roles, of course I use a different name. I can't take the chance that some producer has been cruising my site an hour earlier.'

'What do you think?' Melanie asks her, pointing at me. 'Do you think he's going to get cast or is he going to wind up like Ron Jeremy, doing porn?'

'Well, he definitely has a unique look about him,' Nikita replies. 'You never know.'

It's time for Melanie to put up or shut up, I tell her after we leave Nikita's pad. I give her 48 hours to make something happen.

'You know publicists don't actually get people auditions,' she responds. 'It's usually an agent or a manager who does that for an actor. But they won't work as cheap as I do. You'll have to shell out at least 15 per cent.'

'Then find me an agent,' I demand.

The next day, she schedules me an appointment with an agent named Cara, who runs her own small, independent agency in West Hollywood.

When I arrive there, I notice that the walls of her waiting room are plastered ceiling to floor with framed photos of her clients. Again I find that I am impressed. I am thinking maybe she's the one, until I study the photos more closely and realise once more that I don't recognise a single face. Not very promising, but I suppose beggars can't be choosers.

When I'm finally ushered into Cara's office, she immediately sizes me up and says I have 'the look', but she doesn't know whether I'm actually marketable in a Hollywood dominated by kids in their

Before I came to Hollywood, I had never acted, not even in my high-school play.

Janice Dickinson, the first-ever supermodel, took my head-shot.
That was what got me noticed by agents and managers.

My first role in Hollywood was in a silent film –
which is how Charlie Chaplin got his big break.

Ron Jeremy told me the only way I'd make it
in Hollywood was by doing porn.

At the Church of Scientology, I posed as a gay actor
trying to be cured of my homosexuality.

While doing an interview at the Scientology celebrity centre in LA, I was followed by a hidden camera. Here, being filmed, is actress Jennifer Holmes, who came along with me for the interview.

Meeting Anna Nicole Smith inspired me to become infatuated with Marilyn Monroe.

I got a shot of Brad Pitt on the red carpet at the *Ocean's 12* premiere.

Catherine Zeta-Jones was the most dazzling person I met on the red carpet.

Sigourney Weaver told me she loved the way I dressed.
'How can you not make it looking like that?' she said.

Ex-Mrs Donald Trump, Marla Maples, giving me
spiritual advice at the New Age book launch.

I also met Melissa Rivers, who marvelled at my
green shirt and gold tie.

'Take classes, work your ass off and if you haven't made it by 35,
give up' was the advice from Brad Pitt. So, to be a success in
Hollywood, I enrolled in my first acting class.

I told the Hollywood Chamber of Commerce
I wanted to be the first actor to get a star on the
walk of fame before becoming famous.

20s. She thinks maybe I can get parts for guys in their mid-30s.

'You have something original about you,' she tells me. 'You have presence and charisma. But can you act?'

'Of course,' I tell her.

She takes out a script from an old '70s TV show that I have never heard of and gives me a reading test.

After I'm done, she pronounces her verdict.

'Only so-so.'

She proceeds to ask me questions about my aspirations. I tell her I want to be like Kevin Spacey. At that, she laughs, but does say I look like him.

She says her roster is pretty full, but she'll call me if anything opens up. Meanwhile, she tells me to read the breakdowns and try to make it on my own. I can take a hint.

Two days later, I attend another appointment with an agent that Melanie had set up for me. Within three minutes, the agent, a married woman in her 50s, is hitting on me. She tells me she can 'make things happen' if I go out with her.

I tell her I don't believe in mixing business with pleasure and get the hell out of there before she jumps me. This is the second time I had been hit on by a woman while dressed as His Highness. Maybe I should change the bow tie to an ascot, I think. Or maybe there's such a shortage of straight men in this town that out of desperation these chicks think they have to try to convert any gay man they meet.

And speaking of desperation, I'm starting to think that if I don't get results soon, I'm going to have to whip out my saxophone and start busking at the Hollywood Farmer's Market to raise money for my return plane ticket, following my imminent sacking.

7

★ Silent Sunset ★

'Who do you think I am, Charlie fucking Chaplin?' I yell into the phone.

Melanie had just called to tell me she had finally got me a movie audition. I was excited until she informed me it was for a silent movie.

'It's a legitimate film,' she tells me. 'Silent films are making a comeback and are considered very trendy now. There's even a movie theatre in Hollywood that screens nothing but silent films.'

I'm still very sceptical, but I promise her I'll attend the audition to see what it's all about. It's scheduled for the following week.

'OK, now that you have an actual audition, maybe it's time you learnt how to act,' she tells me.

'I know how to act,' I respond. 'I had the Scientologists convinced I was a gay king! They were ready to convert me.'

'Even the best actors in Hollywood take acting lessons. Brad Pitt goes practically every day. So does Halle Berry, and she won a goddamned Oscar, for Chrissake,' she replies. 'You need an acting coach.'

The following morning, I arrive at the Sunset Boulevard studio of Vincent Chase, a friend of Melanie, who has coached Harrison

Ford, Bill Paxton and a number of other stars. He has agreed to a meeting to give me some tips.

As I'm sitting in the waiting room, killing time while Chase finishes a class, a guy named Carl looks up from his magazine, walks across the room, smiles and sits down beside me. He introduces himself and tells me he likes my outfit. Before long, he asks me if I want to go out clubbing with him that evening. I give him a noncommittal answer but, a few minutes later, he tells me his father used to work for Michael Douglas and that he himself occasionally worked as a gofer for the star. Sensing an opportunity for some good Hollywood dirt, I agree to go on my first-ever gay date. Of course, he would have to show me videos of Paul Newman having a gay orgy with Robert Redford and Steve McQueen to entice me to actually sleep with him, but you never know.

When he finally ushers me in, Chase tells me the best piece of advice he can give me if I'm going to make it is 'act naturally, be yourself and don't overact'. For this, people pay him thousands of dollars? No wonder neither Ford nor Paxton had ever won an Oscar, I think to myself. To be fair, he also tells me that the only way to become a great actor is to study constantly and attend acting classes regularly. He offers to let me attend a few classes when he starts a new session the following month.

My 'date' with Carl starts out more promisingly. He doesn't have anything quite so juicy as the aforementioned video, but he does take me to Hollywood's oldest gay bar, The Spotlight, which is something of an experience. The place is out of a '40s film noir. It is actually quite seedy, though Carl assures me it's considered ultra hip. Which raises the inevitable question: do any celebrities come here?

Carl lists a who's who of Hollywood gay royalty who have been seen in The Spotlight, some quite regularly, but all before they became famous.

'It's too well known for any of them to take a chance coming here now, especially these days, when everybody has a digital or cellphone camera. They'd be outed before they even got home with whoever they'd picked up that night.'

'Name names,' I demand.

He lists about nine or ten well-known actors who he said used to go there. 'Ask the bartender if you don't believe me,' he suggests. I do, and he confirms everything, adding three more names of his own.

'[Young movie star] even gave me a handjob in the rest room four years ago before he did [moderately successful Hollywood film],' Carl adds.

He also tells me that he has got at least three small TV parts by 'blowing the casting director'.

'It's the fastest way to success in Hollywood,' he assures me. 'And don't be fooled, the casting couch is used more often for boys than girls these days. I suspect a lot of straight guys have even sucked cock just to get a role. Hey, whatever works, right?'

I ask him if he would ever sleep with a female casting agent to get a good part.

'Yuck! Never!' he says, with exaggerated disgust. 'But I suppose I'd eat pussy at a pinch. But the role would have to be really good. Like I'd practically have to be guaranteed an Emmy nomination.'

I ask him if Michael Douglas was gay.

'Naw, he was actually quite a womaniser when I worked for him,' he says. 'That was before Catherine Zeta-Jones. Maybe he still is, who knows.'

After a couple of hours, he suggests I go back with him to his Echo Park apartment complex, where he says we can go swimming. I wonder if 'swimming' is a euphemism and politely decline, telling him I have an audition in the morning.

Which isn't entirely a lie. Melanie has actually booked me a screen test for an infomercial for the following afternoon. It is for something called the American Success Network. When she told me about it, I couldn't have been more indifferent; in fact, I outright refused at first. But she said it would be good practice for my silent movie audition, scheduled for the following Tuesday.

When I arrive at the studio, there are about 90 people lined up to audition. Eventually, a guy goes through the line and tells about three-quarters of us to go home: they don't have the 'right look'. It reminds me of the scene in *Schindler's List* where the Jews are separated off the trains, some to live, some to be exterminated. I assume I am about to be unceremoniously told to leave; after all, I'm wearing my outlandish outfit which surely doesn't fit their 'look' – I'm wondering why I even wasted my time coming down. But three hours later, I'm still there.

Finally, this black dude brings me into a room.

'You're here for an infomercial,' he tells me. 'What's with the bow tie and green shirt?'

'It doesn't work for you?' I ask.

'I'm asking you.'

'For me, it works,' I say.

'I'm wondering about your thought process,' he counters.

Thinking quickly of a rationalisation, I say, 'Well, for me, success is what I'm wearing. Green has a lot to do with success, the colour of money. Gold, that's what every American strives for. There's a lot of thought that's gone into this. I appreciate your comment, but I think it works.' (YouTube)

Who is this bozo? I'm wondering.

'What's your role here?' I ask. 'I don't even know who you are.'

'My friend, you're talking to the executive producer of the project,' he replies.

A few minutes later, he tells me to wait outside until I get called to read.

Melanie, who's witnessed the whole exchange, takes me aside. 'You need to change,' she says. 'He's not going to take you seriously and this is very important. He said he didn't like what you were wearing.'

'He said I have potential and that he might want to work with me.'

'Yes, but he didn't like what you are wearing and . . . I'm sorry, I apologise, maybe it is a little too flashy for this part.'

'Don't worry, I'll get the part, and I'm not changing,' I say.

She finally relents. 'OK, so let's work on the script, let's memorise it.'

I'm called into a room with a cameraman, a white screen and lights. The producer tells me to do a run-through.

I do a take: 'Dreams are important. We all have them. Dreams are different than goals because dreams have no time limit. True opportunities happen when you turn opportunities into realistic goals so you can achieve and prepare yourself for the opportunities that come your way.'

Sounds to me a little like the nonsense I heard at the Scientology centre. For a split second I think maybe they're on to me and have lured me into their lair with this infomercial guise.

The producer stops me. 'You have a great look, without the green shirt and the bow tie,' he says. 'You can easily sell this product, but I have to show this to the other partners who are investing in the project. But the reading wasn't great, I will tell you honestly. Still, out of all the guys I have seen, I'd like to see you back tomorrow. I haven't done my callbacks yet.'

Meanwhile Melanie has arranged for me to attend a class at a place called the Hollywood Acting Studio, with a coach named Eric Stone, who has appeared in a number of feature films and TV shows.

When I arrive at his studio, Stone immediately mentions my shades. 'You're indoors now,' he tells me. 'Don't you think you might want to take them off?'

'I think it adds an air of mystery,' I say. 'I like to leave them on.'

There are six of us in his class. The first thing he tells us is: 'With acting, I can tell you for sure, trust the process: it's the process that gets you there, not thinking of the result. Most often we're worried about the scene, worried about the content, worried about what's going to happen.'

Then he splits us into pairs and has us do a scene from a prepared script. When it's my turn to read with a young actress, she seems a little taken aback by my outfit.

'Just picture him the way he is,' Stone tells her. 'You know, no green shirt, no bow tie, no glasses. Just as a regular guy.'

After we finish our scene, Stone says, 'By the way, next week we're all wearing sunglasses and a gold bow tie.' The class cracks up with laughter. (YouTube)

'I like your ideas, you're an interesting guy,' Stone tells me, before I leave. 'You just need to find yourself.'

'Do you think I have a chance of making it as an actor?' I ask.

He hesitates. 'Well . . .'

'Just watch,' I tell him, before he can pour water on my ambitions. 'I'm going to be the most successful of any of your students. You'll have to post a sign outside your studio advertising that this is where I got my start.'

He doesn't seem convinced, for some reason.

Melanie, however, is practically gushing. 'You've helped him so much. I feel so much better right now about what we're out here to do,' she tells Stone, as we get set to leave.

On our way out, we see somebody I recognise from British television, the actor Barry Humphries, better known to many as Dame Edna Everage. He is not dressed as *his* alter ego, but I am dressed as *mine*, so I decide to ask his advice.

'Hey, Barry,' I shout, 'do you think I have a chance to make it as an actor?'

He tells me he likes the garb. The only thing he doesn't approve of is my shoes. 'Get something a bit more glam,' he advises.

This coming from someone who makes Liberace look like Bart Simpson.

At the audition for the American Success Network, I had met an actor by the name of Tony. Melanie seemed to know him and when she introduced me as His Highness, he was clearly intrigued. I'm sure he thought I was genuine royalty. He told me he knew every star in Hollywood. 'I'm probably the only guy who has ever been to all their homes at least twice,' he boasted. I asked him how he knew everyone, but he was evasive. I took his number and he said we should meet up later for a drink.

That night, we meet at the Bungalow Club on Melrose. After a few drinks, he starts to talk. He tells me about all the stars he has met over the years, including Marlon Brando, Charlie Sheen and Robert De Niro. After I tell him a couple of royal fibs – one about how Princess Di used to be a regular at my parties with Dodi Fayed – I manage to gain his confidence. But I really hit the jackpot when I falsely tell him I once snorted a line of coke with Di on my palace roof. Bingo! Tony starts to talk.

'That's how I know everyone,' he says mysteriously.

'What do you mean?'

'Come with me on my rounds Wednesday night and I'll show you,' he says.

At the appointed time, Tony and I drive up to some of the biggest mansions in LA in his brand-new black Porsche SUV. At each stop, he points out who lives in the house and asks me to wait a few minutes while he makes his delivery. Tony, it seems, is the personal drug dealer to the stars. In his glove compartment, he has plastic bags full of cocaine, pot, designer drugs and crystal meth.

'You know all these actresses and singers who look like skeletons,' he says. 'It's meth. That's the secret. It kills your appetite for days at a time and lets you lose 20 lb fast. You always read in the tabloids about how this actress or that one is anorexic because they look so skinny; the real truth is that they are on crystal meth. The funny thing is that their publicists encourage the anorexia rumours because it's not as damaging as the true story.'

He tells me the name of one Hollywood stylist who supplies all her female clients with meth as part of her all-inclusive package. 'I wish I had half as much business as she does,' he says. 'The fact is that she's a shitty stylist, but none of her clients seem to care.'

He says that his most popular and profitable product, however, is not the traditional illegal drugs but rather pills – painkillers and sedatives – which account for more than 75 per cent of his business. He tells me he is referred to around LA as 'the medicine man'.

'The women need them because it reduces the pain of looking in the mirror and seeing all their plastic surgery,' he jokes.

He tells me that he has many celebrity clients, but the majority of his buyers actually work in the business behind the scenes: directors, screenwriters, studio execs. Indeed, only two of the houses we go to that evening are owned by people I have heard of.

After making the rounds for about three hours, Tony takes out a wad of cash from his pocket, around 20K. 'Not bad for a night's work,' he says. 'And it's all tax-free. Now the stars have enough candy until tomorrow.'

A few years earlier, while writing my book about Kurt Cobain, I had spent a lot of time doing research in the Seattle 'shooting galleries' frequented by Kurt and his friends, so I wasn't all that taken aback by this eye-opening foray into Hollywood drug culture. But it did give me an idea.

The next evening, I decide to relive the last night of River Phoenix, who had notoriously died in 1993 of a heroin overdose at the age of 23 on the pavement outside the Viper Room, a Sunset Boulevard club once part-owned by Johnny Depp. Phoenix had starred in one of my favourite films, *Stand By Me*, and at the time I was quite shaken up by his death.

When I show up at the Viper Room around 9 p.m., there is already a line forming to get into that night's show. In my His Highness outfit, I suddenly pretend to collapse on the pavement. Everyone crowds around me, including a paramedic who rushes to the scene. I open my eyes, telling everyone I'm OK, that I'm a diabetic and forgot to eat before I came. One Swedish actress in the crowd named Sanna rushes over to console me and tells me how bad she feels for me. I tell her I felt like I would be the next River Phoenix and that her touching my hand is like Sleeping Beauty coming to the rescue.

I spent the next four days at her pad on Fairfax being consoled by her and watching some of the Swedish porn films she has starred in. Unfortunately, she also cooked me Swedish food and I ended up getting a nasty case of food poisoning.

I almost joined River Phoenix for real.

A few days later, I meet the director of the silent movie, a woman named Samantha Lockwood, at a Hollywood sushi restaurant. Melanie had actually found the listing on Craig's List, under 'auditions', so I'm a little surprised at the setting, as I thought this was going to be a formal audition.

When I see her, I can't believe how hot she is, a cross between Drew Barrymore and Alicia Silverstone.

With introductions out of the way, I ask, 'How do I get the part?'

'You get the part by . . . I have to like you, I have to get to know you.'

'I'm your slave, I'm an actor,' I tell her.

'Well, you're my slave, but I have to like you and I want you to feel like this is a working relationship,' she replies. 'I mean, I can only do the job if you like me and you want to do the job with me.'

She asks me where the whole His Highness thing comes from. I tell her that my family are Cohens, Kohans in Hebrew, which means king; we're considered among the Judaic elite. 'I'm not kidding you. The Cohen is considered King of the Jews. Christ was a Kohan. That's why the Romans called him King of the Jews. Not that I have a messiah complex or anything.'

'I like it,' she says. 'It's kind of a submissive thing to call you His Highness.' (Most people seemed to call me His Highness rather than the more logical 'Your Highness' – probably because I always introduced myself as His Highness Halperin.)

'I'm really hungry for this. I really want this part,' I tell her.

'Do you really?'

'I really do.'

'Let's see,' she says. 'Take off your glasses. Let me see your eyes.' (YouTube)

By this time, I really do want the part. Before meeting her, I had done some checking up on Samantha and discovered that she actually had some Hollywood credentials. She had appeared in the film *Anger Management* with Jack Nicholson and Adam Sandler as well as a bunch of other films and TV series. But more impressive than her own résumé were the acting careers of both her parents. Her father happens to be Gary Lockwood, the star of Stanley Kubrick's *2001: A Space Odyssey*, one of my favourite films of all time. How cool is that? And just as cool, maybe cooler, he starred in not one but two films with Elvis Presley. Her mother happens to be Denise DuBarry, who appeared in Peter Sellers' classic flick *Being There*, not to mention two classic cheesy '70s TV shows, *Charlie's Angels* and *The Love Boat*.

Samantha hands me three pages of script and asks me to read with her. When we are finished, she offers me the part right there and then. When she tells me most of the film takes place in bed and that she is auditioning actresses to play the female lead, I immediately turn the tables on her. I tell her I'll only agree to act in her film if she plays the female role. What better way to get Samantha between the sheets, both literally and figuratively.

Improvising on the spot, I give her a sales pitch.

'There's this whole new trend in independent film for directors to star in their own films,' I bullshit.

When she says she'd prefer not to, I get up from the table and tell her to have a good life. A minute or two later, she chases me onto Sunset Boulevard and tells me she'll do it.

Shooting on the film starts two days later. I spend two entire days in bed with Samantha, having the time of my life. More than once, the assistant director actually has to smooth the bedsheets over me, thinking there is a crease. The truth is, I'm incredibly turned on by the beautiful woman lying half-naked next to me and the lump is no crease.

Before the filming began, I had a bit of a falling out with Samantha after I showed up with my cameraman, Miles. I'd already wasted a number of golden opportunities to capture my adventures on film for my documentary and I wasn't about to miss my acting debut. But Samantha said one camera was enough and asked Miles to leave. Panicking, I told her if he went, I went. I argued that I was documenting my whole experience in LA and needed him on set. Again, she said no. Then I came up with a hook. I told Samantha that Miles's father used to work on the TV show *The Rockford Files* (true) and that he was thinking of putting up a few million to develop silent films because of the recent trend (false).

'He wants to view our behind-the-scenes footage of the shoot,' I explained, 'to see how it all works.' When Samantha heard this, her eyes lit up and she agreed to let us shoot.

I was thinking my part in the film would be a piece of cake, since it was a silent flick and there were no actual lines to memorise, but, in fact, we still had to speak and act as if it was a talkie. And at the same time, we had to wring every ounce of emotion into our facial expressions and body language because that's what the audience would see. (YouTube)

Melanie spent the entire two days on set watching the filming. As she drives me back to my hotel after shooting is finished, she turns to me and says, 'All right, you did a lot better than I expected. I expected shit from you.'

'The bottom line,' I respond, 'is that you saw me on set now, you saw me deliver, you have all the confidence in the world, you're going to get me into the big casting directors' offices, right? I want to win that Oscar, I want to give birth to an Oscar within the next 24 months.'

'Whoa, whoa, whoa! We're taking a leap here. This was a stepping stone, OK? Let's make a deal. You win an Oscar, I get to come with you.' (YouTube)

While she is editing the film a week later, Samantha calls me and tells me the footage is 'incredible'. She invites me out to Malibu that weekend to meet her father and to have a barbecue.

While I'm there, I chat to Gary, who has a lot of stories about Hollywood. He still seems a little bitter that his once burgeoning film career had stalled years earlier. 'One day everyone wants you and the next day nobody returns your calls,' he complains.

It turns out that we actually have something in common. Coincidentally, he had met Samantha's mother, Denise, while filming a TV pilot in the place where I live in Quebec, Mont-Tremblant.

He has nothing but good things to say about Stanley Kubrick, whom he calls a genius and his mentor. But, as His Highness, I am more interested, of course, in the King, Elvis Presley himself, with whom Lockwood had starred in *It Happened at the World's Fair* and *Wild in the Country*.

'He was the nicest guy in the world,' Lockwood recalls. 'He was so kind to everybody, from the crew to the extras. And you know, he was a lot better actor than people realise, but the Colonel made him do all these crappy low-budget films.'

'Did you know he was Jewish?' I ask him.

'He was not. He was a God-fearing Christian,' Lockwood replies.

'That's true, but he was actually a Jewish king, like me.'

I tell him a friend of mine had made a documentary called *Schmelvis* that revealed Elvis's maternal great-great-grandmother, Nancy Burdine Tackett, was Jewish. According to Jewish law, that made Elvis a Jew. When he discovered his Jewish roots, in fact, he placed a Star of David on his mother's headstone, which was later removed by Elvis's father when her grave was moved to Graceland after Elvis's death. He also started wearing a Jewish *chai* symbol around his neck; he was actually wearing it when he was found dead in August 1977.

Lockwood seems incredulous. 'Are you putting me on?'

'No, I'm absolutely serious. They went to Memphis with a crazy rabbi and a Chasidic Elvis impersonator who goes by the name Schmelvis and they tracked down his old upstairs neighbour, the wife of an Orthodox Jewish rabbi. She told them that Elvis and his family lived for years downstairs from them in the heart of Memphis's Jewish neighbourhood. On the Sabbath, the teenage Elvis would act as a *Shabbos Goy*, turning on the stove and the electricity for them, because Orthodox Jews are not allowed to operate electricity on the Sabbath. That's before Elvis found out he wasn't a goy.'

The revelation still hasn't appeared to sink in with Lockwood, who once again repeats, 'Elvis was Jewish?'

'In the film,' I continue, 'the old lady said Elvis was always a wonderful boy and that his mother wanted him to be a doctor, but his grades weren't very good. She also revealed that Elvis had a nose job. And let's face it, if that doesn't prove he was Jewish, nothing does.'

Lockwood laughs, but again repeats, 'Elvis was a Jew? You guys really are everywhere!'

8

★ Collecting for Mel Gibson ★

It's funny that Gary Lockwood mentioned at our dinner that Jews were everywhere because the same subject came up in a different context only a couple of days later. I was having lunch with a TV scriptwriter named Ron whom I had been referred to by Vincent Chase. Up to this point in my film, each time I had been asked by somebody why I call myself His Highness, I had offered a different explanation. So, naturally, when this guy asks me the same question, I give him a variation of an answer I have used previously.

'I'm a Cohen, which in Hebrew means King of the Jews,' I tell him. 'And since I've heard the Jews control Hollywood, I figured it would give me a leg-up in the movie business.'

Without a trace of irony, Ron, who is not Jewish, replies, 'The Jews do control Hollywood, but that's a good thing.'

'How so?' I ask.

'Well, first of all, Jews don't literally control Hollywood. They used to run all the studios, but now there's a lot more corporate control than there used to be, although most of the studio heads are still Jewish, not to mention literally thousands of scriptwriters, producers, directors, etc.'

Even though I'm sure what he's saying is true, this kind of talk is making me a little nervous. I know that for decades the American right has vilified Jews for supposedly controlling Hollywood. The darling of American pre-war fascism, Charles Lindbergh, once gave a famous speech in Des Moines, Iowa, accusing Jews of 'pressing' America into the Second World War through their control of the media, motion pictures and radio. It was almost a carbon copy of a speech that Nazi propaganda minister Joseph Goebbels had given on German radio a few weeks earlier. In fact, Jews controlled less than 2 per cent of the American media at the time, as they do today. But they did literally run every Hollywood studio.

'So why do you say that's a good thing?' I ask Ron.

'Don't you see? It's not the fact that they're Jewish that matters, it's the fact that they're all liberals. As a result, liberal values get instilled into just about every movie and almost every TV show. It's the antidote to conservative propaganda which would otherwise seep into every corner of the country and every young mind. If it wasn't for the Jews in Hollywood, the Republicans would never lose the White House. Abortion would probably be banned. Nobody would ever talk about global warming or racism or oppose the war in Iraq. Thank God for you people.'

It's an interesting perspective. But I'm even more surprised at his next statement.

'Of course, you can't discount the influence of the gay mafia,' he adds.

This is a term that I'm actually familiar with. A few years ago, my old literary agency, Artists Management Group, was headed by Michael Ovitz, formerly the world's top super-agent and later president of the Walt Disney Company. After Ovitz was fired by Disney, he did a famous interview with *Vanity Fair* magazine in which he blamed the 'gay Hollywood mafia' for his demise.

Ovitz told the magazine he was convinced he was the victim of a well-orchestrated strategy led by the openly gay DreamWorks executive David Geffen and his former CAA partner, Ron Meyer. He also singled out Barry Diller, chairman of Vivendi Universal, as well as his former Disney boss, Michael Eisner. He then took swipes at a slew of former colleagues, some of whom were not actually gay and others who had not yet come out.

Needless to say, the town, not to mention the gay community, went apoplectic.

'It really reeks of the homophobia we saw in the '70s and '80s, when a lot of gay execs were closeted,' Scott Seomin, media director of the national gay rights organisation, GLAAD, said at the time. 'This is really surprising and comes off as a bit paranoid, a bit schizophrenic and very homophobic.'

And while Ovitz became the most hated man in Hollywood overnight, his interview underscored a fact that had been whispered about for years: that many of the most powerful players in Hollywood were in fact openly gay.

'So, who actually controls Hollywood, the Jews or the gays?' I ask Ron.

'Take a look at those names,' he replies. 'They're not just gay, they're also Jews. But again that's good, because homophobia is the only bugaboo left in America. Hollywood has done an amazing job in recent years of piercing through the widespread homophobia that always existed in this country. They're the only ones left to counter the Christian right.'

He points out that every year Disney World hosts a 'Gay Day', when thousands of gays and lesbians and their families come together to celebrate gay pride. The company was also one of the first in America to offer benefits to the partners of gay employees. These gay-friendly policies prompted the Southern Baptist Church, the largest Protestant denomination in America, to vote for a boycott of Disney and its products.

'But if you look at the polls,' Ron says, 'Americans are more and more accepting of gays and lesbians every year. Thank Hollywood and the gay Jewish mafia for that. Face it, if the conspiracy theories are going to circulate anyway about Jews and Hollywood, we might as well celebrate the conspiracy instead of pretending it doesn't exist.'

And besides, it's not a conspiracy, it's just a natural by-product of the Jewish tradition of social justice. It makes me proud to be a king of the Jews.

Speaking of Jewish gay-friendly celebs, I just happened to have a meeting scheduled with Roseanne Barr, the outspoken American TV comedian. I was flabbergasted to discover within moments of meeting her that she is Jewish. Who knew?

Our meeting was supposed to be arranged by Prentice Lennon, who thought Roseanne would love the whole His Highness schtick. Lennon failed to get me the meeting, though, so I staked out Roseanne from a position nearby her home and finally met her shopping on the main strip of Bel Air.

Roseanne's television and stand-up persona is a white-trash working-class hick – not exactly one of the many stereotypes associated with us 'Chosen People'. But when we meet in a café near her home, she tells me that she grew up 'like a fish out of water' in a lower-middle-class Jewish family smack dab in the middle of Utah, the Mormon capital of the world.

I tell her I've followed her career for years but that not for a minute would I have suspected she was a Jew. Does she keep her religion low-key on purpose, I ask her.

'Well, in this town, lately it's not such a good idea to advertise your Judaism,' she says. 'You never know whose family thinks you run the world.'

I have no idea what the hell she is talking about until she explains that the fathers of not one but two Oscar-winning A-list superstars, Kevin Spacey and Mel Gibson, are both Holocaust deniers.

'I'm not making that up,' she assures me. 'It's not a joke.'

It seems that Spacey's father, Thomas Fowler, had been a dyed-in-the-wool member of the American Nazi Party until his death a few years earlier. Kevin's brother Randy had recently given an interview to the *Daily Mail* in which he revealed that their father regularly railed against Jews at the dinner table and collected Nazi memorabilia. He had once made Randy quit Scouts because the troop leader was Jewish. Randy also claimed that his father had raped him. When he became an actor, Kevin Spacey took his mother's maiden name and severed all connections with his father.

As for Gibson, his father Hutton and his stepmother have in recent years become the world's most prominent Holocaust deniers, largely because of the celebrity of their son, which offers Hutton a giant media soapbox.

I later discovered that Hutton had given interviews to the *New York Times* and to WSNR Radio in which he'd said that the Holocaust was 'greatly exaggerated' and that many Jews who were allegedly Nazi death camp victims had actually fled to countries such as Australia and the United States.

'It's all – maybe not all – fiction, but most of it is,' he said, arguing that the gas chambers at Auschwitz and other death camps were not capable of exterminating as many people as claimed. 'Do you know what it takes to get rid of a dead body? To cremate it? It takes a litre of petrol and 20 minutes. Now, six million of them? [The Germans] did not have the gas to do it. That's why they lost the war.'

He also claimed Jews were behind a massive conspiracy involving Jewish bankers, the US Federal Reserve and the Vatican.

And, not surprisingly, he has claimed that the 11 September terrorist attacks were not carried out by Islamist terrorists aboard planes but by an unknown party using a remote control.

Roseanne had plenty of dirt to dish on other stars but asked me not to use it until they 'deny the Holocaust or come out of the closet as Republicans'.

Roseanne's brilliant landmark US television show of the '80s and '90s, *Roseanne*, was the first American TV show to portray gays and lesbians in a sympathetic light, so I knew she'd appreciate my undercover investigation as His Highness. Sure enough, she is gleeful when I tell her about it.

'I just thought you had unusual fashion sense,' she says, looking over my outfit. 'I didn't know you were supposed to be a flaming queer. That's brilliant. It's about time somebody exposed the homophobia in Hollywood. It's so sad. Do you know how many of my friends can't ever have a real relationship? Think about it. Can you imagine living your life having to sneak around to prostitutes every night? And if you do find a partner, you live in constant fear that the paparazzi are going to jump out of the bushes and take a photo of you boinking.'

Coincidentally, only a few weeks after Roseanne filled me in on the crazy views of Hutton Gibson, his son Mel was involved in an incident which proved the apple doesn't fall very far from the tree.

On the evening in question, Gibson was stopped and arrested for drink-driving near his home in Malibu, California. According to the leaked police report, Gibson became abusive upon being arrested and stated to the arresting officer, 'Fucking Jews . . . the Jews are responsible for all the wars in the world.' He then asked the officer if he was Jewish, saying, 'You mother fucker. I'm going to fuck you,' telling the deputy that he 'owns Malibu' and that he was going to spend all his money to 'get even'. Later, at the police station, he was videotaped asking a female officer, 'What are you looking at, sugar tits?'

When the media got wind of the incident, it prompted howls of outrage both inside and outside Hollywood. Amazingly, many of the reports quoted Gibson's friends and supporters saying how shocked they were to learn that Gibson would say such things about the Jews.

Frankly, I was shocked that anybody could be shocked. Maybe they didn't remember a little film old Mad Max did a couple of years ago called *The Passion of the Christ* which blatantly portrayed the Jews as bloodthirsty savages who killed his Saviour. It was a nasty piece of work and although Gibson always denied it was anti-Semitic, most Jewish leaders and gentile theologians disagreed.

It seems that Gibson belongs to a fringe element of Roman Catholicism that believes the Vatican came under Satan's grip during the Second Vatican Council, which his father Hutton Gibson has frequently claimed was a Jewish plot to destroy the Catholic Church. Like his father, Mel's brand of ultra-conservative Catholicism also rejects the reforms of the Vatican Council that liberalised the Church in the early '60s and he practises many forbidden rituals that had been outlawed by the modern Church, such as the Latin mass, before Pope Benedict restored the ancient tradition in 2007.

According to Hutton Gibson, 'The Jews are after one world religion and one government. That's why they've attacked the Catholic Church so strongly, to ultimately take control over it by their doctrine.' He said former Federal Reserve chairman Alan Greenspan, who is Jewish, should be lynched: 'Greenspan tells us what to do. Someone should take him out and hang him.'

And it seems that Mel Gibson shares some of his father's views about the Federal Reserve. In a 1995 *Playboy* interview, he hinted cryptically that a number of presidential assassinations have been retribution for economic reforms that challenged the powers that be: 'There's something to do with the Federal Reserve that Lincoln did, Kennedy did and Reagan tried,' he said. 'I can't remember what it was. My dad told me about it. Everyone who did this particular thing that would have fixed the economy got undone. Anyway, I'll end up dead if I keep talking.'

So does Mel actually disavow his father's views? Yes and no. While he has acknowledged that there were many atrocities committed against the Jews by Hitler (which even Hutton has acknowledged), he constantly refuses to come out and say he believes there were six million Jews exterminated by the Nazis.

In one interview with *Reader's Digest*, he said about Hutton: 'My dad taught me my faith, and I believe what he taught me. The man never lied to me in his life.' In another interview, he told *The New Yorker*: 'I don't want to be dissing my father. He never denied the Holocaust; he just said there were fewer than six million. I don't want them having me dissing my father. I mean, he's my father.'

And in an interview with ABC reporter Diane Sawyer after his drink-driving arrest and anti-Semitic rant, Mel said he would not allow 'detractors . . . to drive a wedge between me and my father. I'm tight with him. He's my father. Gotta leave it alone, Diane. Gotta leave it alone . . . We're talking about me right now, and me taking responsibility for my words and actions. And . . . I'm certainly not going to use him to sort of put anything off on me.'

But Sawyer persisted. 'Even if it's the explanation for what happened that night?'

'It isn't the explanation for what happened that night. It isn't. It has nothing to do with it. It's . . . that's in my own heart,' he said.

When Sawyer asked him about his hateful comment that night about the Jews, he responded, 'Let me be real clear here. I don't believe that Jews are responsible for all the wars in the world. That's an outrageous drunken statement.' Still, he maintained that the Jews were 'not blameless' in the continuing Arab–Israeli conflict. And he admitted that his hostility towards the Jews might have been triggered by lingering resentment for charges of anti-Semitism he took in the aftermath of *The Passion of the Christ*. 'I had my rights violated . . . as an artist,' he told Sawyer.

Of course, he said this in a country where the majority of people believed Bush when he claimed Iraq had weapons of mass destruction, so I have no doubt that millions of the ignorant masses will swallow the idea that he's not actually anti-Semitic. It was the alcohol, of course, that said these things, not him.

My friend Max Wallace is currently working on a documentary called *The Survivor and the Star*, exposing what he calls Gibson's 'true nature'. Max has known Gibson's personal priest, Stephen Sommerville, through family friends for more than a decade and he claims in the film that Sommerville has made outrageously anti-Semitic remarks to him over the years, including the bizarre assertion that the Jews control the US government. The controversial priest, who was suspended by his former Canadian diocese for his views, also questions the accuracy of the Holocaust and believes, like Hutton Gibson, that the figure of six million Jews exterminated is widely exaggerated. He also told Max that the Jews are the 'enemies of Christianity. It says so in the Bible.' Interestingly, Gibson flew Sommerville to the set of *The Passion of the Christ* to say mass for him and the crew while the epic was being filmed in Italy and has recently hired him as his full-time parish priest in Malibu.

As the recently anointed His Highness, King of the Jews, I decided it was up to me to avenge my people.

I read about Gibson's anti-Semitic rampage on the celebrity website TMZ.com, which broke the story, and figure it is time to take matters into my own hands. I decide to drive up to Malibu to see if any of Mel's neighbours share his views.

When I arrive, I station myself in front of Ralphs grocery store on the right side of the Pacific Coast Highway in the Malibu Colony Plaza and hold out a bucket with a sign over it which reads: 'Free Mel Gibson – A Victim of Another Jewish Conspiracy'. This sets off fireworks. Dressed in my His Highness outfit, people come up to me all day, agreeing with my campaign and telling me how poor Mel deserves a better fate. One elderly woman in her 90s, who tells me her husband used to 'own Hollywood until them Jews invaded', says, 'Son, you have even more courage than Mel for standing here and putting yourself out there. Most people agree with you, but no one has the courage to stand up.' She gives me $40.

Wow, I think, this is turning out to be a profitable venture. I decide I will use whatever money I make to treat myself to dinner at the best restaurant in Beverly Hills. I imagine how pissed off Mel will be to know a royal Jew has had the night of his life on him, as he emerges from his jail cell.

Next, one man comes up to me and gives me a huge hug and a $20 bill. 'Thank you, it's about time somebody stands up. For years them people have invaded us like flies. The media never mentions that – instead they lock up innocent Mel. Personally, I'd ban them folks from here. All they do is drive their fancy cars around to show off how well they've done. They're all a bunch of bastards. Hitler was evil, but he was not stupid in trying to get rid of them.'

Amazingly, only two people question what I'm doing. One Jewish couple stops and the husband says, 'C'mon, do something more productive with your life. Mel Gibson finally got what he deserved. It's shameful that you're out here supporting him.' Another person threatens to call the cops on me, saying, 'You're promoting hatred.' I retort, 'Freedom of speech, freedom of speech. I have nothing against the Jews, but they've got to stop picking on Mel.'

To be fair, most people who support my campaign aren't necessarily anti-Semitic, but they tell me Mel's a 'good guy' with a drinking problem. Many of them know him personally from living in the same community. After three hours of standing outside Ralphs, I've raised more than $300. When I return to LA, I have the best meal of my trip and then drink all night at the bar of the Roosevelt Hotel – all thanks to Mel.

Meeting Roseanne was great, but she was after all only a sitcom star. I needed somebody with a little more Hollywood credibility to give my film some gravitas. I needed to interview a genuine movie star, especially if I was going to sell the film in international markets, where big names attract attention. So I put out feelers to the contacts I had made to date and, within a few days, Prentice Lennon calls and says he will try to arrange a short interview with Brad Pitt. You can't get much bigger than that, and I was excited at the prospect.

But after I'm put in touch with Pitt's people, and go through days of phone calls and tentative promises, I'm finally told that Pitt is 'unavailable'.

I'm quite disappointed at this setback until Vincent Chase, the acting coach I had befriended, tells me he can arrange an interview for me with one of his clients, Bill Paxton. Not quite in Pitt's league for glamour but still a movie star. Paxton, it turns out, had actually starred in at least two films that outperformed most of Brad Pitt's films at the box office, *Twister* and *Apollo 13*, as well as co-starring in the blockbuster *Titanic*.

When I learn this, I think, 'This guy's a player. His advice will be nothing to sneeze at.' I am actually excited as I arrive at Chase's studio, and find Paxton waiting for me. Within minutes of our meeting, however, I can't help but think he's trying to tell me something about my quest to make it in Hollywood.

'I get a little resentful of people who think they can just waltz right on in,' he says in a very genial tone. 'It never ceases to amaze me when people go, "Well, I can act." But really, it's like, would you say, "Oh sure, I can perform this appendectomy," or "Go get a coffee, I'll land this 747."' (YouTube)

He proceeds to lament the state of today's Hollywood. 'Films today are not what they used to be,' he complains. 'They don't look as natural. Maybe because of technology. If you look at old movies, it was all done in one or two takes, making it look much more natural and convincing. Actors today don't have to be great. Back in the day you had to command your craft to be in the movies.'

- ★ -

I haven't mentioned to this point that I actually have a tenuous Hollywood connection in my family. Andrew Walker, who starred for a couple of seasons in the popular TV show *Sabrina the Teenage Witch*, as well as the movie *Wicked Minds*, is the brother of my ex-wife. He currently lives in LA as a struggling actor. When I set out to make my film, I was actually hoping he would be my entrée to Hollywood, and he did indeed agree to be interviewed. (YouTube) He hadn't really helped much in terms of connections; however, one night he made up for it when he got me invited to a *Playboy* party at popular hotspot the Sunset Room, on North Cahuenga Boulevard.

When I arrive as His Highness, practically every *Playboy* model in the place is all over me within 15 minutes. They seem to think I'm royalty – based on people at the party referring to me as 'His Highness' – a misconception that I do little to disabuse. Normally, this would be my dream come true, but the place is also crawling with real celebrities and I don't want to waste the opportunity. In fact, Cameron Diaz comes up to me at one point and asks all about my background and royal lineage. After we toast a shot of vodka together, she gives me a huge kiss on the cheek, telling me how honoured she is to meet a Jewish king. Cool.

Next I bump into Mark Wahlberg, who seems like a super nice guy, very down to earth. We talk about the current state of digital film and we both agree that in five years most theatres will have digital projectors. When I ask him for advice, he says to get the best manager possible if I want to make it as an actor. I enquire who his manager is, but he is not very forthcoming. 'You wouldn't be given the time of day,' he says.

During the course of the evening, I see people snort coke in corners, walk in on a couple having sex in the men's bathroom and I even see one short, stocky guy put two guns in his coat pocket. I am a little disappointed that there is no sign of Hugh Hefner, though two different people assure me he'll show at some point.

Sure enough, around 10 p.m. there is a commotion across the room; Hef has arrived with three gorgeous blondes, who somebody tells me are his 'girlfriends'. They are accompanied by two huge guys, who I presume are bodyguards, who act as a barrier between Hef and the rest of the crowd. He is dressed neither in his familiar smoking jacket nor in pyjamas but in a blue sports jacket. He is looking quite old and I wonder how he can keep up with three women, none of whom appears to be older than twenty-five. I mention this to a guy at the party who is also watching Hef's arrival with interest.

'One word,' he says with a grin. 'Viagra.'

Finally, a voluptuous *Playboy* model with the biggest silicone chest I have ever seen starts hanging around me after a friend of hers points me out, telling her that I am royalty. She introduces herself as Jenny.

Jenny is all over me, telling me her lifelong dream has been to marry Prince William but that meeting a Jewish king is 'even more exciting'. I'm thinking she's completely whacked. She tells me she knows everyone in Hollywood.

'I've dated every star under the sun,' she says, though I find it hard to believe. 'Some of them were even married. They're all full of crap. That's why I'm so happy to meet a real person like you. I am so honoured to be in the company of royalty.'

Before the night is over, I end up in the back of Jenny's Saab convertible, drinking a Martini while she gives me the Monica Lewinsky treatment. The perks of going undercover, I think to myself.

Probably the weirdest moment of my entire foray to date, in fact, happens in this car. At one point, Jenny insists I spill my royal seed all over the seats.

'I want you to bless this car, His Highness,' she says. 'From now on, whenever I sit in here I'm going to feel like I'm sitting in royalty.' I decline her invitation, but she won't let me back into the party unless I promise her a trip to the royal palace, which I've told her is in Tel Aviv. 'No problem,' I assure her. 'I'll have Mr Sharon send you a private jet. But I'll do it in a few weeks because I want you to find a local rabbi and take Hebrew lessons. It's a courtesy that is asked of anyone planning on visiting me at my royal palace.'

Three weeks later, I get a call from Jenny. 'Shalom, His Highness,' she says. 'I'm ready to come to the palace.' She has not only taken Hebrew lessons but also joined a synagogue in Bel Air. Wow, I could convert the masses with this His Highness story. I tell her the palace is under renovation because a suicide bomber had recently pulled up and tried to blow up the place, thinking I was inside.

Back at the party, I run into a somewhat familiar face who has also heard that I am some kind of royalty. It turns out that she is a former *Playboy* centrefold, a woman by the name of Anna Nicole Smith. It is past midnight and Anna Nicole has just arrived. At the time, I didn't actually know a lot about her, just that she was famous for being famous. I had actually watched about ten or fifteen minutes of a reality TV show she had starred in a couple of weeks earlier while flipping through the channels in my hotel room.

She seems a bit out of it, but, like Jenny, she appears to be completely infatuated with my royal connection At one point, she tells me she'd love to marry into the royal family. I'm not sure if she's proposing to me or if she means the British Royal Family, but I may have pursued the notion a little further if I'd known at the time that she stood to inherit almost $1 billion from the estate of her late husband, J. Howard Marshall, the octogenarian old coot who keeled over shortly after marrying Anna, undoubtedly because she wore him out in the boudoir.

I saw her another four times, though I never got to visit the *Playboy* mansion, where she promised to take me. The first night, at a sushi bar, she took me outside and suggested we do a couple of lines of coke together. Amazingly, her son Daniel was sitting right next to us when she asked. I declined but was left wondering what kind of mother this loose cannon actually was. I was surprised at how little attention we attracted when we were out in public, though at this stage the public's obsession with her had not yet really started. Only once did anybody take her picture, though she did wear sunglasses in public and usually had her hair covered in a kind of scarf, so it was difficult to recognise her.

We agreed to meet two days later, for a late-night coffee at the Urth Caffé in Beverly Hills. Anna, dressed in a revealing tank top and jeans, told me all about her tragic life. And about her problems with men.

'I can't really find the right guy,' she said. 'Everyone just wants to fuck me. That's why I like you, His Highness – because you didn't put the moves on me the first time we met.' Or perhaps she actually believed hooking up with me would gain her access to the crown jewels. Little did she know that the only jewel I had to my name was the gold earring I wore as an act of teenage rebellion when I was 16 designed to piss off my mother.

We spent the next hour writing poetry together. Anna would write a line and then I'd finish it. One of the poems was about love, and I still have it – at least until I sell it on eBay:

Follow me,
To Ecstasy.
Follow me,
to the square surrounded by flowers.
Follow me,
Till the end of time.
Follow me,
And dance cheek to cheek till the end of life.

Around 11 p.m., Anna asked me to do her a favour. She wanted to go hang out at the gravesite of her idol, Marilyn Monroe. I agreed, thinking it could be fun. We hopped into my rented Dodge Durango SUV and Anna directed me to Marilyn's resting place at the Westwood Village Memorial Park. When we arrive, the gates are locked. Anna, however, says she hangs out there all the time and knew a part of the cemetery where you could hop over a fence to get in. I tell her I am afraid of being arrested for trespassing, but she says not to worry. We hop over the fence and Anna gives me the grand tour, pointing out everyone's grave from Fanny Brice to Truman Capote to Walter Matthau. When we arrived at the grave of Natalie Wood, Anna yells, 'She was fucking murdered.'

She tells me that Wood was mysteriously drowned one night after falling overboard from a yacht while the only other occupants, her husband Robert Wagner and Hollywood bad guy Christopher Walken, were supposedly sleeping on board. She never tells me which one she suspects of committing the murder but insists that what she has told me is, in her opinion, true.

Finally, we come to where Monroe is interred in a pink marble crypt at the Corridor of Memories, #24. 'This is the same cemetery where her foster mother, Grace Goddard, was buried too,' Anna says. She then told me all about the funeral, about how Joe DiMaggio, Monroe's ex-husband and loyal friend, claimed her body and planned her service. She describes how Joe excluded anyone he deemed morally responsible for her death – which was just about everybody in Hollywood. Judy Garland was one of the 32 invitees and she sang 'Over the Rainbow' at the chapel. For years after, until his death in 1999, Joe would arrange for fresh flowers to be placed in front of the crypt.

Anna, who, like Monroe, is a former *Playboy* playmate, points to the crypt next door and tells me that Hugh Hefner had bought it for his own remains so that he could be buried next to Marilyn for eternity.

'Hef told me lots of neat stories about her,' she recalls. 'I think he's even more obsessed with her than I am. Of course, Marilyn was his first ever pin-up and she helped make him rich.'

Then Anna tells me that Monroe was buried in what was known at that time as the 'Cadillac of Caskets'. It was manufactured by the famous Belmont Casket Company, she says, seemingly cognisant of every bit of obscure trivia about Marilyn's death.

'Whitey Snyder had done her make-up, because she made him promise to do that if she died before him. Monroe held a small bouquet of roses and was dressed in her favourite green Emilio Pucci dress.'

Then, to my surprise, Anna repeats verbatim the eulogy that Monroe's acting coach, Lee Strasberg, delivered at the funeral. The most powerful section, which Anna recounted emotionally, is the line: 'She created a myth of what a poor girl from a deprived background could attain. For the entire world, she became a symbol of the eternal feminine.'

Then Anna shocks me. She starts to take off her clothes and asks me to make love to her right in front of Marilyn's resting place.

'C'mon, baby, she'd get a kick out it,' Anna says, plunking a huge kiss on my lips.

For the first time in my undercover investigation, I cannot resist, thinking to myself how many men would kill to make love to Anna Nicole Smith in front of Marilyn Monroe's gravesite.

'Marilyn is looking down on us with a big smile,' she says after we finished.

This isn't actually my first intimate encounter with a celebrity. When I lived in England, I briefly dated the actress Julie Walters and also a granddaughter of Winston Churchill. But it is the first time I have ever slept with a former *Playboy* playmate and it is definitely good for my ego.

Two years later, when I learned of Anna Nicole's death and the paternity challenge filed by Larry Birkhead for Anna's daughter, Danielle Lynn, I wondered for a brief second if maybe I was the father (I was never very good at maths). When the results of the paternity test were finally announced and Larry Birkhead told the press, 'The DNA says I am 99.9999999 per cent the father,' I thought to myself, 'Hmm . . . what about that other .0000001 per cent?'

Interestingly, during the peak of the brouhaha about the paternity of Dannie Lynn, it emerged that Prince Frederic von Anhalt, a member of the Hungarian Royal Family and the husband of Zsa Zsa Gabor, had claimed that he'd had a decade-long affair with Anna Nicole and that he might actually be the father.

Evidently Anna's attraction to me was based neither on my looks nor my charm but her obsession with royalty.

My brother-in-law Andrew figures in another interesting Hollywood-related anecdote concerning royalty, dating from before I set out to make my documentary.

In about 2000, when I was still married to Walker's sister, Andrew had landed his starring role in the made-for-television movie *Wicked Minds*. He was to play opposite the former *Sports Illustrated* swimsuit supermodel Angie Everhart, who was once engaged to Sylvester Stallone. In fact, according to Angie, one of the main reasons for her break-up with Stallone was that during Angie's breast implant surgery he walked in and ordered the doctor to make Angie's breasts even bigger – while she lay there unconscious. In a trial against the doctor, it was claimed that Stallone had told him he wanted them to be 'big but perky, kinda like a 17 year old' and the doctor apparently complied against Everhart's wishes.

When Angie, then 32, first came on set, she told Andrew, then 20, she wanted to hang out with him every night because it was his town and he knew the hotspots. In fact, they did more than hang out.

They spent almost every night together in her room at the luxurious Vogue Hotel in Montreal.

One night, I went out for drinks with Andrew and Angie and got to know her. Angie told me about how difficult it was for her to find a boyfriend. I looked at her as if she was nuts. She complained that guys wanted to sleep with her only because of her looks and celebrity but never wanted to commit.

'Prince Andrew calls me all the time,' she said. 'He definitely wants to fuck me. He's an example of a guy who prefers sleeping with redheads. He loves redheads.'

I took this revelation with a grain of salt and, though I didn't tell her so at the time, I found it very difficult to believe. However, years later, in May 2007, it was announced that the Prince was dating Angie. In fact, when she accompanied Andrew as his date to a Windsor Palace ball in honour of his daughter's 18th birthday party, the British tabloids wrote that Angie looked exactly like a younger, thinner version of his ex-wife, Fergie.

Ironically, Prince Andrew also figured prominently with another person I was peripherally associated with, Courtney Love, who claimed that the Prince showed up unannounced one night at her LA home and demanded she let him in. Of course nobody believed Courtney's story until Buckingham Palace issued a confirmation of the incident but denied that the Prince had a romantic interest in the former junkie.

Angie talked at length that night at the bar about the obstacles of dating celebrities. 'The problem is, if you're both celebrities it will never last,' she told me. 'Most of these relationships are prearranged by the stars' managers. They want so-and-so to be with so-and-so in order for all the paparazzi to film it so everyone gets a ton of publicity. The only marriages that last in Hollywood are the ones where the couples lead separate lives.'

Which brings me to the subject of my biggest fan, Jackie Collins, who has written a number of bestselling novels on the topic of Hollywood relationships. I had the idea that Collins would be perfect to talk about these and other Hollywood-related topics in my film, so I decided to contact her. After Jackie named my book *Bad and Beautiful* as her book of the year in 2002, I had sent her a large bouquet of flowers in thanks, which led to a friendship of sorts. It also led to her literary agency – Janklow & Nesbit, one of the largest in the world – agreeing to represent me for my next book.

I reached Collins' publicist, Melody Korenbrot, who promised me she'd ask Jackie to be in my film. A few days later, Melody got back to me saying Jackie would love to appear in the film but had a few conditions. First, she wanted the interview to be conducted in a suite at the Beverly Hills Hotel. 'I don't want to fuck her, I just want to interview her,' I told Melody. Second, she needed $900 for hair and make-up. This was actually more than my monthly salary at the time. I told Melody I needed to capture Jackie in a natural state, not all dolled up like the characters in one of her novels. Shortly afterwards, Jackie sent me a message through Melody telling me she was honoured to be asked but that it 'probably would not work out'. She told Melody that if I was in a jam, she'd do it down the road.

I never got back in touch with her because, frankly, I did see her point. She's a star and deserves to be treated like one, rather than like Dan Di Julio or the other struggling actors in my film who were in no position to demand anything more than bottled water and a Dunkin' Donut.

9

★ Crashing the Oscars ★

I was beginning to think my film was getting a little self-indulgent. Who was going to want to see a film about a schmuck like me? Here I was in supposedly the world's most glamorous town, filled with the most famous people on earth. This is what people want to see in a film about Hollywood. If I was ever going to put asses in the seats, it was time to give the people what they wanted.

Ever since I changed the focus of my film to an undercover exposé of Hollywood, I had thought about crashing the Oscars. What bigger stage worldwide than the planet's largest entertainment extravaganza? The glam, the glitz, the fake boobs, the Botox, all in one place.

And I had just the plan. At every Oscar ceremony, there are a couple of hundred non-celebrities chosen to be seat-fillers whose role is to quickly occupy a seat when an invited guest gets up to go to the bathroom. The idea is that the camera must not show any empty seats when it pans over the audience.

I was determined to secure one of these coveted positions and to use the opportunity to get unprecedented publicity for my film. I would wear a tux to the ceremony over my His Highness costume. With some categories every year, you see eight or nine people associated with a winning film going up to bask in the glory, so when a nearby group of attendees got up to accept their award, I would also get up onstage then reveal my green shirt and gold bow tie. My plan was actually to make my move during the presentation of one of the minor awards, when I'd be less easily detected. By the time anyone realised the weird guy with the shirt and bow tie onstage to accept the Best Special Effects award wasn't actually an Oscar winner but instead some scam artist out to promote his forthcoming Hollywood documentary in front of more than a billion viewers worldwide, it would be too late for anybody to do anything.

I still remember watching the Oscars as a child the year a streaker raced past David Niven while he was presenting onstage. More recently in 1991, the year *The Silence of the Lambs* was nominated, a gay-rights group announced that they had more than 50 people in the audience who were planning to make a scene if Jodie Foster won the Oscar for Actress in a Leading Role. They claimed that the film was homophobic and didn't like the fact that Foster, who it is rumoured is a lesbian, had failed to speak out about the negative portrayal of gays. Foster did indeed win the statuette, but there was no scene, possibly because the group had broadcast their intentions in advance, sparking unprecedented tight security inside the auditorium.

But I wasn't going to make the same mistake. They wouldn't know what had hit them until I had already done my thing and was being dragged out by a battalion of bouncers. It wouldn't win me any Oscars, but it would guarantee worldwide publicity, probably a distribution deal for my film and a lot of dough in my pocket when the press descended on me afterwards and wrote about my documentary-in-progress. Maybe I'd even get some appearances on the late-night US talk shows.

I had got the idea for the prank after a guy I met named Jeremy told me he had worked as a seat-filler at the ceremony for the previous four years. In the beginning, he told me, you had to apply to an outside company and be interviewed, but now the Academy of Motion Pictures chose their own seat-fillers based on internal recommendations. Jeremy said he would put my name forward after I had promised him that I would use him in my film, though I didn't tell him about the stunt I had planned.

I waited and waited for the invitation to come, but I didn't ever hear anything. Jeremy assured me he had recommended me but had also not heard anything back from the Academy.

On the afternoon of the Awards ceremony (the Awards take place early on the west coast so that they will be seen on the US east coast during prime time), I arrive at the Kodak Theater in my rented tux. The crowds are already in the bleachers to watch the red-carpet arrivals and the atmosphere is electric. I've attended World Cup football matches and even a Super Bowl game, but nothing in my experience even comes close to the Oscars for glamour and excitement.

I approach the woman at the security gate and ask her where guests who arrive on foot are supposed to report. She directs me to a cordoned-off area, where two security guards wait with clipboards. I give my name.

'You're not on the list,' the guy tells me.

'There must be a mistake,' I reply. 'I'm a guest of Kevin Spacey.'

'You would have received an invitation, which you need to show to get in,' comes the reply.

'Don't you know who I am?' I say haughtily. 'I am His Royal Highness Halperin, King of Israel and its dominions.'

'I don't care if you're the goddamn Queen of England. No invitation, no entrance.'

I end up watching the ceremony at a nearby bar, where I hold court as His Highness, telling the assembled patrons that I have an invitation to the ceremony but prefer to be with the little people, my royal subjects.

When the ceremony ends, I head over to Morton's steakhouse to try to crash the *Vanity Fair* party, where all the Oscar winners congregate afterwards. I am determined to get a photo of His Highness holding a genuine Oscar statue, as it will be a perfect image for the film's promotional poster. The security here is even harder to penetrate than at the awards gala itself. This time, I announce that I have been hired to serve drinks. I am immediately ushered to the back of a giant tent, where another list awaits me, along with no fewer than 20 security guards and a massive array of LAPD officers. Again, I am told to scram when my name fails to appear on the list.

'Who's in charge here?' I whine. 'I have six children at home who are counting on my wages from tonight in order to eat.'

'If you're not off the premises in ten seconds, those kids will be without a daddy because you'll be spending the night in a cell,' says a guy in a tuxedo, who appears to work for the restaurant.

Thwarted again.

Up to this point, the celebrity pickings in Hollywood have been sparse. Other than my interviews with Roseanne Barr and Bill Paxton, and my intimate encounter with Anna Nicole Smith, my biggest celebrity sightings have been Keanu Reeves, Jamie Foxx and George Clooney.

I happened to bump into Reeves at a small grocery store on Yucca in Hollywood. He was a very nice guy and obviously knew the staff because they were all on first-name terms. I truthfully told him I liked his band, Dogstar, and he was flattered, though I failed to tell him that I wasn't as impressed with his acting, which always struck me as resembling the gruntings of Neanderthal man. When I told him I play sax, he went on and on about how he loves the sax. When an adoring young girl came up to him, he was only too willing to sign an autograph.

It was another story meeting Foxx, whom I encountered in a

restaurant on Melrose. He was full of himself and possibly the rudest, most arrogant person I met during my whole stay in LA. When I went up to him, he refused to talk and I didn't even manage to say anything before I was shooed away with a wave of his hand. One of his posse immediately got up and gave me the eye, making it clear I should stand back. When four curvaceous women approached him a little later, however, he was as nice as can be.

The one celeb I seemed to keep bumping into, no matter where I went, was Clooney, who appeared to be omnipresent. I had first encountered George outside the Formosa Café on Santa Monica Boulevard back in 1998. He looked fit, was wearing Converse running shoes and was with two gorgeous model-types. He was in a great mood.

'George, I like your Chuck Taylors,' I said. 'I guess it gets the women.'

'Probably does,' he responded. 'I thought it was my hair, but you have made me re-think.'

The next time I bumped into him I was back in Montreal and he was directing and shooting *Confessions of a Dangerous Mind*, about the game-show mogul Chuck Barris. I saw him several times that summer – at a health club, at a bar, at a coffee shop and walking downtown. Everywhere I went George seemed to be there. I started to wonder if we were stalking each other.

Interestingly, a good friend of mine from my musical days, Cha Cha Da Vinci, was then a successful talent agent and was hired by Clooney to provide actors for the film. She got more publicity than she ever bargained for when George started having an affair with one of her young stars, Maria Bertrand, who George spotted when Maria brought him a glass of wine as she worked at Globe, a trendy restaurant in Montreal's Plateau Mont Royal. Enamoured with Maria, he offered her a part in the film alongside his all-star cast of Drew Barrymore, Matt Damon and Julia Roberts. Someone leaked the story to the tabloids and a media frenzy ensued. The couple were stalked by the paparazzi everywhere they went. My ex happened to be good friends with Maria, who confided to her that she was in love with George, who, before meeting her, had been seen almost every night having lap dances at Montreal's most famous strip club, Chez Parée.

My next Clooney encounter came a couple of years later while travelling by plane from Montreal to LA. Through the doors came George, wearing a Yankees baseball cap. He spent the entire six-hour flight reworking a script.

'George, I keep bumping into you everywhere I go,' I told him after we arrived in LA and had disembarked from the aircraft.

'You look familiar,' he said. 'Are you an actor?'

'No,' I told him. 'I hang out at strip clubs a lot.'

Embarrassed, he politely said, 'Have a good day, nice meeting you.'

Clooney's film *Ocean's 12* was set to premiere at LA's Kodak Theater and everyone from Brad Pitt, Bruce Willis, Julia Roberts, Sharon Stone, Matt Damon and Michael Douglas was scheduled to attend. I was determined to get in. But how? My efforts to date in crashing star-studded events had been embarrassingly inept. But my publicist Melanie comes up with just the plan.

She passed by the theatre in the afternoon, wearing a low-cut top and a miniskirt. Immediately, two security guards hit on her, though when she told them she wanted to see the show that night but didn't have a ticket, they tell her she is out of luck.

'What about just the red carpet?' she asks. They tell her she can only get on with a media pass. She asks them to show her one, so they take one out. Then she asks if she can take a picture of them holding it. One of them obliges, asking her for her phone number. She gives him a bogus number and promises to meet up later that evening for drinks. Immediately, Melanie runs to a nearby Kinkos copy centre with her digital camera and develops the photo, in which she has focused only on the press pass, reading: 'Red Carpet Access Only'. She proceeds to get it blown up and laminated, and makes two duplicates, one for me and one for Miles.

'See how far a good pair of boobs gets you in this town,' Melanie says, as she presents me with our magic passes, which look completely authentic. Talk about chutzpah.

It works like a charm. First, Melanie strolls on, then a few minutes later I walk right on with Miles, casually strolling by the massive security, flashing our phoney passes. As the stars arrive and wave to the crowd, I'm right there attempting to chat them up. (YouTube) Although whenever I approach a celebrity, a publicist or handler practically accosts me and tells me to 'keep back'. Still, it's exciting rubbing shoulders with the stars: His Highness Halperin walking in the hallowed footsteps of Hollywood royalty.

And although our pass doesn't permit us to watch the film, I wait until it's over to see if I can possibly score an interview with any of the stars leaving the cinema. Sure enough, I finally get my interview with Brad Pitt, who I ask for advice about becoming an actor.

'Take classes, work your ass off and if you haven't made it by 35, give up,' he tells me. 'Oh, I guess you're already over 35. What can I tell you?'

A couple of weeks before I left for Hollywood, I'd had a dream that I got offered a role in a new Dom DeLuise film. The studio wanted someone to replace Burt Reynolds in an attempt to revive DeLuise's career, which had floundered since he came to fame playing Reynolds' sidekick in films such as *Cannonball Run* and *Smokey and the Bandit*. In my dream, I was starring in an action movie playing a pool hustler and DeLuise was my bookie. We were two Americans who move to Moscow and outmanoeuvre the Russian mob. When I woke up, I was disappointed that it was only a dream and that I still had to try to land a movie role for real.

Ironically, a month later I was hanging out in DeLuise's apartment with actress Jennifer Holmes, who had rented his condo in Beverly Hills. 'It's great dealing with him,' she said. 'He's a great guy and keeps everything up to par – as long as you pay the rent on time.' I tried to persuade her to introduce us, thinking I might get some good dirt on his old friend, Burt Reynolds, but Jennifer was reluctant.

- ★ -

Since arriving in Hollywood, I had seen more than my fair share of drugs – people sniffing coke, people smoking joints, etc. – but I had no idea how much of a problem drugs were in Hollywood until I am invited by my friend, the actress Jill Gold, to an exclusive party at a house in the Hollywood Hills.

Lots of familiar faces are there, including Britney Spears, a few members of the Los Angeles Lakers basketball team and a lot of lesser-known B-list actors who I don't recognise but who are pointed out to me throughout the evening. People are partying as if it's their last day on earth.

One actress named Carlene and I get into a heated conversation about George Bush. She's a huge Bush supporter, which is kind of weird in Hollywood, supposedly the heart of the liberal establishment, but I'm later informed by Melanie that 'young Hollywood', with some notable exceptions, is completely clueless, concerned more with partying to excess than current events.

Speaking of clueless, Britney, who I see across the room for a total of less than two minutes all night, is wearing a red see-through top with a black bra sticking out. She is also wearing a short black skirt with high heels. This, of course, is before she had children, so she hasn't yet let herself go and is looking pretty hot. I can't tell whether she has come with a date because she spends most of the evening in the basement, which has been designated a VIP area, where I am most decidedly not invited or welcome.

This concept of the VIP room, somebody explains to me, is a relatively new phenomenon. In the old Hollywood, the stars attended each other's parties, where commoners were rarely to be found. But in recent years, a number of trendy clubs have pioneered the concept of a special room segregated from the rest of the establishment, where celebrities and other high-profile personalities can party without fear of being accosted by autograph seekers, stargazers or paparazzi. This way, everyday people are willing to shell out a huge cover charge so they can say they party at the same club as this or that celebrity, even though they are lucky to even catch a glimpse of somebody famous. In order to attract celebrities to their establishment, club owners arrange for the star and their entourage to be treated like VIPs, ensuring the booze is flowing freely all night, including unlimited bottles of Cristal champagne.

Another relatively recent phenomenon is the concept of the paid party animal. Under this scheme, a club owner will actually pay a celebrity to show up at their party, guaranteeing a certain level of glamour. Apparently such appearances, which can net a celebrity anywhere from $10,000 to $100,000, are negotiated with written contracts that specify how much time the celeb must spend hobnobbing with the masses. They are paid extra for such perks as spending time in the DJ booth spinning music for the crowd. Of course, most A-list celebrities don't need the money and consider it beneath them to accept any requests to appear at a party or club. So it is usually a B-lister who gets recruited for such events. The most notorious professional party animal is Paris Hilton, who has elevated the concept to an art form and is said to earn as much as $1 million a year for showing up at parties.

A few weeks after they separated, I actually bumped into Britney's ex, a notorious paid party animal, and he seemed like a nice guy. He did have a gorgeous girl hanging off him, but he was very polite and

141

approachable. I asked him about his split. 'You know, you just gotta move on,' he said. 'Some things work, some things don't.'

Back at this particular Hollywood Hills party, I am introduced to everyone as 'His Highness'. One person who does not seem at all captivated by my schtick is the singer/actress Lindsay Lohan, who has been informed that I am 'royalty'. Lohan, who spends most of the party in the VIP room but also mingles with the main crowd for quite some time, just looks at me, without any emotion. Either she has seen it all before or is completely stoned out of her mind. Though I don't witness her doing any drugs at the party – one of the few who doesn't imbibe openly, at least in our section of the house – the following year she checked herself into rehab.

And, although she is widely known for her penchant for leading men, she seems to be at the party with a woman who looks old enough to be her mother. Lohan has bragged to friends in the past that she has slept with stars such as Jude Law, Joaquin Phoenix, Jared Leto and James Franco.

'She's probably slept with them all,' says Doris Redmond, an aspiring actress at the party, who stared in awe at Lohan. 'I believe her. It's probably her who leaks it all to the press for publicity. Lindsay pretends she hates the tabloid press, but she actually relishes it. She'd be nowhere without the paparazzi.'

And though Paris Hilton does not show up this particular night, I actually bump into her months later at a club on the Sunset Strip. The place is blasting house music and a lot of minor celebs are there, including sports star Dennis Rodman and the rapper Ice T. Paris is decked out in a skimpy red dress that barely covers her privates. One thing I notice is her toes; Paris has got to have the nicest feet in Hollywood, I think. Later, at the bar, I tell her so and she just smiles and says, 'Thanks.'

Another time, I am walking with a private eye named Tom Grant when we spot Paris with her pal Nicole Richie in front of The Ivy restaurant on North Robertson. She is smoking a cigarette. Tom yells out, 'Better stop that, Paris, or it will stunt your growth!' She looks at him as if he is crazy.

- ★ -

One of my best sources in Hollywood turned out to be a guy named Moby. Moby had been homeless in Hollywood on and off for 12 years until he started selling illegal DVDs on the street. Since then, he tells me, he's made a small fortune because he is able to sell DVDs before the films actually come out in theatres. The most shocking thing about his story is how he gets advance access to the films: from the studio execs themselves. Moby said he befriended one of the most powerful execs in Hollywood, who'd give him copies of the film to watch before it came out. Moby used to be an assistant director and is an avid film buff, and the exec was so impressed with his knowledge of film that he'd given him an advance copy to screen.

'He thinks I'm sitting there in my living room watching the thing by myself,' he laughs. Little did the exec know that Moby was actually making hundreds of copies with sophisticated duplicating equipment and selling them on the street, and sometimes even to other markets, like New York and Philadelphia.

'I was running an empire until the cops clamped down,' he says. 'They made it tough for me.' Moby claims that the LAPD shelf other crimes, like homicide and mugging, to chase low-life criminals like him. 'That's how powerful the studios are here and how much clout they have with law enforcement. I was never arrested but pressure was put on me. One time I gave a cop an advance copy of *Mr. and Mrs. Smith* in exchange for not being arrested.'

Moby says that he now does his deals in a much quieter manner. First off, the people giving him the films are now low-level employees at the studios. He gives them a small cut of the pie. 'I have connections in every studio here,' he said. 'In fact, I also get to read scripts before they come out. I knew how *Rocky Balboa* would end before anyone else, except for Mr Stallone. Literally the day after he finished writing it, I had it in my hands through a source who Stallone gave the script to for delivery to Sony.'

Moby, however, isn't the only one who uses technology for illicit purposes. Shortly after I changed the focus of my project to an undercover Hollywood exposé, I decided that the most sensible way to go undercover and document the experience would be to use a hidden camera. I had once worked behind the scenes on an investigative news show for Canadian television which frequently used hidden cameras to expose corporate skulduggery, so I was familiar with the concept.

I asked my cameraman, Miles, for advice on using similar methods in LA and he took me to a store in Studio City which specialises in the technology and frequently rents sophisticated hidden cameras to reality shows such as *Survivor*. Because my budget was a tad smaller than theirs, I had to settle for a small unit that consisted of a camera and a microphone hidden in a red tie and a baseball cap, while the receiver remained in a car nearby. I felt like James Bond the first time I put it on and visited a talent agency, and it actually worked quite well, although the video image left a lot to be desired. Unfortunately, after a few more tries, I discovered from Tom Grant that such technology is actually illegal in the state of California and I wouldn't legally be able to use any of the footage in my film. This discovery nearly derailed the entire project as originally I had envisioned filming the whole documentary clandestinely. I briefly considered shelving the whole project and just writing a book instead. But I decided to press on and instead come up with creative ways to justify filming my adventures through legitimate means, including obtaining signed releases from all my subjects.

Most of the hidden-camera footage I had to shelf was uneventful anyway, but there was at least one classic moment that I was heartbroken to lose. One day, I heard that Governor Arnold

Schwarzenegger was going to be holding a mini-press conference in LA and giving a speech about education. Who better to get advice from about breaking into acting than the Terminator himself, who had, without any discernible talent, turned himself into one of the world's most bankable movie stars before taking on a political career.

So I sat through an interminably boring speech, or perhaps it just seemed boring because I couldn't understand a thing he was saying, as to me his accent still sounds like a cross between his character, Conan the Barbarian, and his father, the SS officer. At the conclusion of the presumably weighty speech, I jumped to my feet along with the rest of the press corps and shouted out, 'Governor, what advice would you give a person like me, attempting to make it as an actor in Hollywood?' Like the consummate politician, he pretended to ignore me and pointed to another reporter. But I could swear I saw him grin before he blew me off.

I was walking along Rodeo Drive one day when I thought I was about to have my biggest celebrity encounter to date. I saw a guy who, from an angle, looked exactly like Paul Newman. He turned out to be a down-and-out actor in his late 60s named Roman. He told me that he'd had a burgeoning career until about 25 years ago, when he was blacklisted for sleeping with both the wife and the daughter of a studio head, though not at the same time.

'First I did the wife and no one found out,' he says. 'Then I did the daughter and fireworks erupted. I've never worked again.'

In honour of Newman, I took Roman to a supermarket and bought him a gigantic Caesar salad and a bottle of Paul Newman salad dressing called Newman's Own. While we eat in a nearby parkette, Roman relates a harrowing story about Marlon Brando.

'He was a pig,' Roman says. 'He used to pay people to beat up writers who gave him bad reviews. I knew him well. If you messed with him, you'd pay for it. There was one writer who trashed him in an article and two days later the writer was seen picking up his teeth on a corner of Hollywood Boulevard. He never wrote about it because the man who beat him up told him that if he did, he'd be picking up the teeth of his four-year-old son next.'

Roman had dozens of stories like this one about other celebrities, but I was never able to figure out whether he was telling the truth or if he was just a crazy old geezer.

I had composed the entire musical score for my documentary and I was ready to lay down some tracks, but I needed a singer for the title song, 'Hollywood'. My friend, Dora, introduced me to a woman from Toronto named Chloe who she said had a voice like molasses. I arranged to meet her at the Roosevelt to see if she was up to the task. During the course of our meeting, she told me she had worked for years at Toronto's best-known strip joint, Brass Rail, before she moved to LA to launch a singing career.

'I've danced for a lot of stars,' she said. 'Samuel L. Jackson has been into the club, and I even danced for Joaquin Phoenix in his hotel room. He was a gentleman and didn't demand sex. He treated me well and paid me close to 2K.'

A few weeks earlier, I had actually met a stripper who called herself 'Sunshine', who also revealed her celebrity sightings. She told me she had danced for George Clooney, Mike Tyson and a man she thought was President Clinton.

'I'm almost 100 per cent it was Bill, because I could see him through his baseball-hat-and-sunglasses disguise and he was surrounded by two men, who looked like secret service agents, even though he wasn't President any more. I danced for him in the VIP lounge for more than an hour and he was extremely kind. He told me he loves black women [Sunshine is a stunning, leggy black 22 year old] and that he thought I was gorgeous. He dropped over 1,000 bucks on me and tipped me $250. I was sure it was Bill, but in this business when someone well known walks in you have to pretend you don't recognise him. A couple of years later, when I saw him on TV campaigning for his wife, Hillary, I couldn't help but think what type of weird relationship they must have. And don't think Bill is too excited about checking into the White House again. Judging by where he keeps his offices [Harlem] and his appreciation for the lap dances I gave him, he'd prefer checking into the "Black House" any day of the week.'

Samantha Lockwood, the director of my debut film, was good friends with Arthur Sarkissian, who produced the box-office blockbusters *Rush Hour* and *Rush Hour 2*, starring Jackie Chan and Chris Tucker. She offered to introduce us. I figured it could be interesting to get the perspective of a Hollywood mogul, so I met up with him at his office on Sunset Boulevard.

The first thing I tell him is that I am considering pitching a documentary about his career, which definitely gets his attention. For the next week, he lets me hang around with him, cruising around LA in his Maserati while he tells me stories about the old Hollywood, though not a lot of good gossip.

'I went into a studio meeting at one point,' he recalls one day, 'and I was talking about [legendary film director] Sam Peckinpah, and the studio executive turned around and said, "Why don't we get him?" and I said, "Because he's dead. He died ten years ago." I'm looking at this guy and I say to myself, what an idiot. He earns $2 or $3 million a year and he doesn't know jack shit . . . The people who run this town now are all a bunch of morons. They have no sense of Hollywood history, no appreciation of who came before.' (YouTube)

We attend a number of auctions because he is a fanatical collector of vintage Hollywood posters and will shell out thousands of dollars to acquire them for his collection. During our time together, he also spends hours on the phone to Hong Kong director John Woo, because Arthur was to produce Woo's next film, *The Red Circle*. He promises to introduce me to John and to get me on the set of the new movie when it begins shooting.

One day, as I am sitting with Arthur at the Elixir Tonics Café on Melrose, a trendy Zen Buddhist celebrity hotspot, Salma Hayek walks in. I introduce myself as 'His Highness, King of the Jews'. Hayek tells me that she is fascinated with Kaballah but isn't quite as enamoured with the Jewish spiritual fad as her friend Madonna, at least not yet.

Another day, we are sitting in Arthur's office when his assistant walks in and tells him 'the deal' is about to 'go down the toilet' because of the 'shitty script'. Sarkissian goes ballistic. It turns out they are in talks about a film Arthur is scheduled to produce with $14 million in financing from the French channel Canal +.

Arthur gets on the phone to his contact at the channel. 'Don't worry,' he tells him, 'I'll put the writer on a leash. He's written for me before. We'll get this done, I promise. You'll love the script when we're through with it.'

When he hangs up, he immediately calls the writer and tells him he better shape up or he's off the project. 'You have one more chance to get this thing done,' he warns. 'I'm not going to fire you, but you have to do it my way.'

I was kind of hoping Arthur would offer me a part in *Rush Hour 3* and I hinted at the idea a few times, but instead he gave me a lot of useless advice.

'You've got to schmooze, schmooze, schmooze if you want to make it in Hollywood. Just be yourself and network.'

Yeah, that and $8 will get me a double-mocha latte at a Starbucks in West Hollywood, I think to myself.

However, Arthur does end up making himself useful a week later when he tips me off about a pool party being thrown by a major studio executive in Santa Monica. When I pull up in the driveway of the opulent mansion, I see that the driveway is full of Porsches, Ferraris and Mercedes, and I am a little embarrassed getting out of my rented SUV and handing the key to the valet.

Inside, the cocktails are flowing. There are mostly hot women and older men, but unfortunately not a lot of actual celebrities. I think I recognise Drew Carey and Carmen Electra.

After chatting with a number of other guests, I am finally introduced to the studio mogul who is our host. The guy's vice president of something or other and clearly a very powerful figure in this town. He has been informed that I am a member of a royal family by a guy to whom I had given the whole spiel and he asks me if I am related to the Queen. He's a Jew and I know I can't fool him with the story of how I am Israeli royalty, since there is actually no such thing. So I tell him instead that I am a Luxembourg prince and that the Queen of England is a distant cousin. He asks me about my stay in LA and wants to know if there is anything he can do for me. I tell him I'm thinking of investing $80 million in a film, but I haven't found the right project yet. DreamWorks is courting me very heavily, I tell him, and I've been wined and dined repeatedly by both Steven Spielberg and David Geffen. Immediately, his eyes light up. He tells me he has a new film in the works and that Brad Pitt is currently reading the script. 'The studio is ready to make Pitt an offer if he likes it,' he tells me. He says if I wanted to invest, he could guarantee me a better return on my investment than any bank or financial institution.

Now he's my best friend and I feel it's the perfect time to ask him the question I have always wanted to ask someone in his powerful position: 'Is it just a myth or does sleeping your way to the top actually happen in this business?' I say this with a mischievous glint in my eye, suggesting the answer I want to hear.

He smiles and puts his arm around me. 'Your Royal Highness [which is what I told him to call me], you see all these beautiful women in this room? None of them would be here if they didn't suck my dick. That's Hollywood. The best part of this business is being around gorgeous young girls all the time and getting them to do whatever I want. And if they don't, plain and simple, they'll never work in this town. Every actress you see on the big screen has got on her knees to get to the top. It's the way it's been since the days of Mary Pickford and it's the way it will be 100 years from now. You think these young dumb nymphos are artists? No way. They're complete idiots who didn't get enough attention when they were young, so they trek to Hollywood to become famous. They have nothing to do with art. Da Vinci, Picasso – those are artists. Not some young fuck with fake tits from Tennessee who can barely tie her shoelaces let alone memorise more than a few lines at a time. So, to answer your question, if they don't swallow my honey, then I don't show them the money.'

My question has been answered, and I think I need a shower after being around this sleazebag.

The studio executive is not, in fact, the slimiest character I meet in Hollywood. That distinction would definitely have to go to a guy I met named Colin, an 'agent' in his mid-30s, who showed me his secret concoction for wooing young girls into his bedroom.

Every hot girl who came to Colin's office would be offered ice tea, which he admitted to me he'd spike with various drugs that were aphrodisiacs, though he said he stopped short at giving them Rohypnol, the date-rape drug, as if that would improve my opinion of him. He'd then invite them out for dinner and they would usually end up at his apartment with them in bed before midnight, all with the unspoken promise of him getting the girl a part, playing on her vulnerability or desperation.

'Let's face it,' he told me candidly, 'anyone who becomes an agent is in it for one thing only – to meet hot girls and get laid. Anyone who tells you different is not being honest.'

Colin admitted to me that he'd been doing this for years and has bedded over 2,000 girls since he became an agent in 1992, though I found this figure a little hard to swallow.

'I get laid more than Al Pacino, Brad Pitt and Nick Cage put together,' he boasted. 'Not bad for a guy originally from Iowa who couldn't even get a date for his high-school prom.'

I asked him if he ever got these actresses parts.

'Sure,' he said. 'Otherwise I'd starve. I specialise in representing talent for TV commercials and lately I've been focusing on recruiting participants for reality shows. The sex is just the icing on the cake.'

Another good source of Hollywood sleaze I met was working as an LA County sheriff's deputy while moonlighting, with the blessing of his police department, as an actor. I met Deputy 'Al' at the second reading for my infomercial (which I eventually failed to land, by the way).

I told him I might have work for him on a major film and he agreed to meet me for coffee at the Urth Caffé on Melrose, which was by then becoming my regular hangout. At first he was reluctant to talk about his experiences as a cop in Hollywood, so I shifted the conversation to the film I was working on getting produced. I told him it was about an LA cop who moonlights as an actor and hits it big after befriending a studio mogul who is illegally running a prostitution ring.

'That sounds like what actually goes on here,' he says.

He opens up after I promise him the part if the film gets produced.

'You wouldn't believe some of the things I've seen in my four years on the force,' he says. 'Half the people in the film business should be in jail, but Hollywood is just too powerful. They act as if they're immune, and they practically are. I know several big names who have raped women or men, who deal all kinds of drugs and molest young boys, and they get away with it. It's not even just us and the LAPD who are to blame, it's the District Attorney's office, who fail to prosecute these cases all the time.

'The O.J. trial actually started to change things around here. If not for O.J., Robert Blake [who was accused and later acquitted of hiring a hit man to kill his wife] would have never been put on trial. He would still be wreaking havoc. The saddest part is if you're a black guy like O.J. you get the book thrown at you. Believe me, there were many people before O.J. who committed gruesome murders, but they got off because they were famous and white.'

He refuses to name names, but tells me that 'one of the biggest actors today, who commands at least $10 million a picture, has been accused of rape at least four times.

'We never lay charges because he's good friends with someone high up. The actor even went to his daughter's 16th birthday party and signed autographs for everybody there only two days after a woman had filed a complaint that he had raped her. She was convinced not to pursue it because it would be his word and his lawyer's against hers. Can you believe that shit?'

By this point, I could believe almost anything about this town.

In December 2004, I attended Kevin Kline's induction to the Hollywood Walk of Fame. It was packed with celebrities. The first one I met was Sigourney Weaver, who shook my hand and complimented me on my garb. 'I love it! Best outfit I've seen in Hollywood,' she said. 'I love the shirt and tie.' I felt like bursting into laughter. Though I was quickly almost reduced to tears when I found out Miles had fallen asleep while filming and forgotten to turn on the camera's microphone. What a golden opportunity missed.

Then came the highlight. Melanie went up to the star of the hour, Kevin Kline, and informed him a king was in attendance at his star ceremony. Kevin's face lit up. He came towards me in a crowd of people and said, 'Pleased to meet you, His Highness.' I replied with, 'Congrats, Kevin. Great job.' Then we shook hands. Thank God Miles woke up and managed to capture this one properly. (YouTube)

The following year at another celebrity-related event, Miles isn't with me, but no harm is done because there are at least five television crews capturing my antics. I was in my hotel room one day when I saw on the news that one of my comedic heroes, Richard Pryor, had passed away. I immediately donned my costume and took a taxi to Pryor's sidewalk star way up on Hollywood Boulevard. When I arrived, there were already about a hundred people placing wreaths and flowers, along with a pack of camera crews and journalists desperately seeking quotes from fans.

Pryor was the ultimate prankster so, in his honour, I decided I would dupe the assembled media. I approached the star on my hands and knees with a bouquet of flowers I had picked up off the sidewalk and cried out, 'Richard, baby! Richard, brother, how could this happen? After all we've been through, brother, and now you leave me all alone. Brother, how could this be?'

Suddenly, every microphone and camera was in my face. 'Please give me space for a couple of minutes,' I said. 'Please drop your cameras while we all say a prayer for brother Richard.' Seconds later everybody assembled had bowed their head while I led a prayer. 'Bless his soul, bless his brethren and bless his spirit – repeat after me . . .' They repeated my words. 'May Richard rest in peace.' And they repeated this again. Then I got up and announced that I was ready for questions.

An ABC *Good Morning America* reporter asked me who I was. I told her I was His Highness, a local LA comedian who owed his career to Richard.

'He hated all the goddamn white comedians except for me,' I said. 'He loved my stand-up. And he loved me.'

'How many shows did you do with Richard?' asks another reporter.

'We toured everywhere – sometimes he even opened for me. He always said there was only one white motherfucker he respected – not Seinfeld, not Milton Berle and not your Aunt Pearl, but His Highness.'

I then shushed the crowd and told them I was ready to proclaim the truth. Absolute silence ensued.

'I'm here today to tell you how racist this business actually is,' I then declared. 'If Richard wasn't born with a tan, his star would be in front of the Kodak Theater in the centre of Hollywood instead of way up here in this seedy neighbourhood. If his name was Gleason, Candy or Hope, his star would be right in the centre of it all. This is a great injustice. Richard opened the door not only for every brother who ever dreamed of telling a joke but also for Jewish comics of royal descent like myself. In fact, I'm challenging every Jewish comedian in LA and New York to *sit shiva* for seven days for brother Richard.'

That night I was sitting in my hotel room watching the local news when suddenly I saw myself ranting at the camera about Pryor's comedy legacy and racism in show business. The caption on the screen read: 'His Highness – Local Comedian'. I'd like to think Richard got a big laugh watching from the sky.

By this stage, it had dawned on me that although I had taken on the His Highness persona as a means of exposing Hollywood homophobia, it was actually a far more useful vehicle for shedding light on the foibles of American celebrity culture.

10

★ Cementing His Highness's Name ★

Of all the great landmarks that evoke the glamour and celebrity of Hollywood, I'd have to say that none is more evocative of the town's golden era than the Hollywood Walk of Fame. The walk spans a three-mile stretch on Hollywood Boulevard, where thousands of pink terrazzo and bronze stars are embedded in the sidewalk, commemorating all the greatest stars of Hollywood, past and present. Or so the Hollywood powers-that-be would have you believe.

Indeed, all the great movie legends are represented there. Each morning, I would take a walk along the Boulevard just to stargaze and to think how cool it would be to have my name down there encased in a star. And then one day, as I was having that very thought, I noticed something unusual. Although most of the stars enshrined in that pavement are unquestionably deserving – including icons such as Marilyn Monroe, Gary Cooper, John Wayne and Bette Davis – I couldn't help but be struck by some of the other names I came across. I stumbled upon the, in my view, vulgar billionaire developer Donald Trump and then a slew of embarrassing game-show hosts, pop stars and bad TV actors. At first, I simply questioned how such mediocrities could be represented there, cheapening the Walk and trivialising the contributions of the true greats. Then it struck me. If Wink Martindale and Trump could have their own stars, not to mention Vanna White, whose sole contribution to show business is turning letters on an American game show, then why not His Highness Halperin?

So I did a little research to determine just how I would go about immortalising myself in concrete. The results were quite enlightening.

It seems that the idea for the Walk of Fame goes back to 1958, when a California artist named Oliver Weismuller was hired by the city to give Hollywood a facelift. Two and a half thousand blank stars were installed along the boulevard and it was up to the Hollywood Chamber of Commerce to choose worthy recipients. The first star to be inducted was the actress Joanne Woodward, wife of Paul Newman, in 1960. In the next 16 months, 1,558 more stars were added to the Walk.

There are apparently five separate categories one can receive a star for, although the cowboy crooner Gene Autry is the only person to have been honoured with all five possible stars.

Four stars have been stolen from the Walk of Fame over the years, including those of Jimmy Stewart, Gregory Peck and Kirk Douglas. That explains the presence of cameras all along the Boulevard, installed to deter more robberies, though the presence of cameras in Hollywood doesn't seem quite as Big Brother-ish as it does in, say, London.

At Hollywood and Vine, there is a special 'round star' on each corner for the astronauts of the first Moon mission, Apollo 11, which I found kind of cool because I had always wanted to be an astronaut.

There are two film actors named Harrison Ford with stars. The first Harrison Ford was a silent film actor between 1910 and the 1920s. The second is the present-day Harrison Ford, of *Star Wars* and *Indiana Jones* fame. Even fictional characters have their own stars, including Bugs Bunny, Mickey Mouse, Godzilla, Kermit the Frog and Winnie the Pooh.

The Walk of Fame has also become a shrine fans can visit when celebrities die or get into trouble. When Michael Jackson was on trial for child molestation in 2003, for example, throngs of fans descended on his star to leave flowers and letters of support.

In recent years, it seems, the Walk has become more of a venue to promote a newly launched album or upcoming film than as a true celebrity tribute. Britney Spears, for example, was awarded her star just as her album *In the Zone* was released and she took the opportunity to hype it shamelessly at the ceremony; Kevin Bacon was awarded his star just as his movie *Mystic River* hit theatres; and Nicole Kidman got hers just in time to generate Oscar buzz for her role in *The Hours*. It worked.

In 2002, the Walk of Fame broke tradition when Muhammad Ali's star was placed on a wall of the Kodak Theater instead of on the sidewalk, at Ali's request, so that he wouldn't be walked on.

Of course, I had no problem at all with being walked on. In fact, it seemed as if people had been walking all over me since I arrived in Los Angeles. The least Hollywood could do was award me a star to make up for it.

I discovered from a number of people that although there is a formal selection committee, the choice is really made by a guy named Johnny Grant, Hollywood's so-called 'honorary mayor' who heads the selection committee. So I don my His Highness costume, draw up a petition to have me awarded a star and head to the pavement in front of the Roosevelt Hotel wearing a sign on my back saying: 'Get His Highness a Star – Sign This'.

Almost immediately I am surrounded by 'fans' – mostly tourists – who clamour to sign the petition. The Japanese in particular are convinced I must be somebody famous. One woman almost faints with excitement. Another woman, from Austria, tells me she recognises me from TV. At least 100 people turn the pen over to me after they sign the petition and demand my autograph. One guy from LA who must have known I was a nobody says I probably deserve my star more than half of the folks who have stars. 'You have the green shirt,' he says. 'You look like a star. And you deserve a star.' (YouTube)

Within six hours, I have more than 1,600 signatures. I'm almost convinced that I will soon receive my star, by popular demand.

The next step is to phone Johnny Grant's office. I tell the woman who answers the phone that I am His Highness, a major star, and have a massive petition from the public demanding that I am awarded a star. She's not impressed. She says she has never heard of me, tells me they don't accept petitions, but informs me that I'm welcome to fill out an application.

I tell her that if they put my star in a seedy, remote section of the boulevard, like Richard Pryor's, I'll protest and boycott the ceremony. I then inform her I will accept a spot in front of the Kodak Theater, but if that isn't available, they can put me on the wall next to Muhammad Ali.

'He used to be the Greatest, but now I am,' I tell her.

In fact, I assure her that if they put my star in front of the Kodak Theater, all my royal friends will attend the ceremony – including the Queen, Diana's brother Charles Spencer, Fergie, Andrew and Prince Charles. And, as an added bonus, Prince William has agreed to give my induction speech. I also tell her that the Queens of Sweden, Jordan and the US will attend the ceremony.

My comment about the US Queen appears to go over her head; unless she thinks I am referring to Boy George, who now resides in New York. At any rate, she promptly hangs up the phone. But I'm still not deterred.

I've heard that in order to be even considered, you have to grovel big-time to the 'mayor of Hollywood', so I make reservations at Morton's for Johnny Grant and myself, using Grant's name, and then call back his office to tell him we'll be dining at eight o'clock on Tuesday. Before the secretary can respond, I hang up the phone.

I know it's a long shot, but I show up at the fancy steakhouse at the appointed time and inform the maître d' that I will be joining Johnny Grant for dinner. He gives me the once-over and tells me that Mr Grant is not there. I tell him I'll wait at our table, but he doesn't seem particularly amenable to that idea, especially since my attire is definitely out of place among the rich and powerful who frequent the establishment.

'You can wait outside for Mr Grant,' he sniffs. Instead, I head back to my hotel, confident that Grant hasn't taken me up on my invitation.

When I drop by the Chamber of Commerce to pick up the application form a few days later, I discover that it will take a little more than some ass-kissing to secure my star. It turns out that a 'sponsorship fee' of $25,000 is required for the 'maintenance' and 'upkeep' of the star. It will be no trouble at all for me to go by a couple of times a week with a broom and dustpan and tidy up my star, I tell the receptionist. Apparently either the movie studio or publicist usually ponies up the fee for their stars, she informs me.

But I still haven't given up.

The next morning, I return to my spot in front of the Roosevelt. This time, I am wearing a sign that says: 'Sponsor His Highness's Hollywood Star'. (YouTube) To each curious passer-by, I explain my plight: but for the lack of $25,000, I could be immortalised in concrete. I offer each person the same tempting deal. For the person who puts up my sponsorship fee, I will tattoo their name on my forehead at the induction ceremony, using the words 'His Highness, sponsored by John/Jane Doe'.

After nearly three hours, I have raised a total of $4.70. Only $24,995.30 to go . . .

But even now, I haven't given up hope. I'm all ready to convince the distributor of my documentary to cough up the money to promote the film. And then I read the fine print on the application form.

In addition to the $25,000 sponsorship fee, it informs me, before a nominee can be considered, he or she must prove that they have 'contributed to the community' through some altruistic cause, like working with the homeless.

This is the final straw. Royalty does not mix with hoi polloi. It's just not done. Or so I inform the Chamber of Commerce in my letter explaining that I am no longer interested in their star and wouldn't accept one even if Marilyn Monroe herself were to rise from her grave and beg me to take hers.

11

★ The Hollywood Ten ★

My film was turning out to be a light-hearted romp through Hollywood, but I was determined not to gloss over the town's dark side. Something told to me by my new friends, the Queers of the Round Table, had initially led me down this path by accident.

While they had been naming names of all the stars who were allegedly gay, one in particular had caught my attention. It was my favourite actor from one of my favourite 1970s TV shows, *The Waltons*, which depicted family life during the Great Depression. The actor was Will Geer, who played the feisty but lovable old grandpa.

'Total fruit,' declared Lenny while we were playing cards that first night.

'But he has a daughter, Ellen Geer, who is a well-known actress,' I protested.

'Hello!' said Lenny. 'Haven't you heard anything we've been telling you? Probably 90 per cent of the queers in this town are married and have kids. Not only was Grandpa Walton a big old fag but he was also sleeping with the single most important homo in American history.'

'Who's that?' I asked, thinking the answer would be Truman Capote, or Liberace, or somebody equally flagrant.

'Harry Hay,' he replied.

I had never even heard the name and told him so.

It turns out that Hay was a very prominent radical activist who founded the first high-profile gay-rights organisation, the Mattachine Society, in Los Angeles during the '50s, calling for the repeal of sodomy laws and other homophobic legislation. He later established another group known as the Radical Faeries.

In the '30s, Hay – who was also married, like most gay men in those days – had met the young Will Geer, who introduced him to radical politics, and they had become inseparable, performing for benefits for exploited workers and in political agitprop theatre.

While I was doing research into Geer, I actually came across an enlightening magazine interview Harry Hay had given to journalist Owen Keehnen in 1992 in which he discussed both Geer and gay Hollywood.

When Keehnen asked Hay what gay Hollywood was like in his day, he said, 'Most places had one naked bulb and you really couldn't see the people across the bar from you. In other words, it was a form of cruising indoors.' Gay Hollywood, explained Hay, was 'a series of very well covered up cliques'.

Asked how he met his one-time lover, Geer, Hay recalled that he was cast in a show called *The Ticket of Leave Man* and the lead actor was Geer. 'Will was so wonderful. I used to sit in the wings every night and just moon over his performance. At that time he was one of those sort of ugly men who could be gorgeously sexy,' he said.

As interesting as it was to learn about Geer's little-known secret life, that's not what intrigued me the most about his story. For my documentary, I had actually been planning a segment outing Geer. I figured that it was unethical to out living celebrities, and it would be kind of boring to talk about gay celebrities without actually naming any, but it would do no harm to out a dead one. So I was mulling over a segment in the film where His Highness outs Grandpa Walton, but I was still fuzzy on how I'd go about it.

I discovered that Geer had built a small outdoor theatre on the outskirts of Los Angeles called the Will Geer Theatricum Botanicum. That's where I was going to ambush unsuspecting tourists and theatregoers with the news, I decided.

When I arrive at the Theatricum one weekend afternoon and start talking to one of the employees, I ask her if she knows Geer was gay. 'Oh sure,' she says, 'although I think he may have preferred women to men. The gay stuff was just part of his left-wing politics.' Then I discover something much more shocking than finding out Geer was gay. 'The ironic thing was that [Senator Joseph] McCarthy was also gay and he's the one who had Geer blacklisted,' says the woman.

'Geer was blacklisted?' I ask sheepishly, aware that I haven't done my homework very well.

'Of course,' she says. 'And he was damn proud of it. He didn't name names like those despicable weasels. That's how this theatre came into existence. Geer started it so that he and other blacklisted actors would have a place to perform.' She also tells me that Woody Guthrie had actually lived there once when he was down and out, and his friend Geer gave him refuge.

It turns out that Geer, who had been acting since the 1920s, had been called to testify before the infamous House Un-American Activities Committee. He refused to give the names of his fellow actors who were members of the Communist Party and, as a result, he could hardly get any work until the 1970s, when *The Waltons* revived his career.

Until this point, the darkest thing I had discovered about Hollywood was its history of forcing gays into the closet. Here was an actor, Will Geer, who had suffered the double whammy of the celluloid closet and the Hollywood blacklist.

I actually don't know a whole lot about the blacklist so I decide to learn more about this period. Unfortunately, there is no museum or memorial commemorating this shameful, dark hidden chapter of Hollywood history and so I have to go further afield. My real goal is to find somebody who had actually been blacklisted, but I know that will be tricky since most of them are probably dead. Vincent Chase refers me to a well-known producer he knows, who is a walking encyclopedia of Hollywood history. So I decide to pay him a visit and see what he knows. It turns out this is one subject he is particularly passionate about.

'I was completely disgusted when they all got up and gave him a standing ovation. Remember that?' he replies, when I enquire about the blacklist.

I haven't a clue what he's talking about. 'Who?' I ask.

'Elia Kazan.'

I vaguely remembered there being some controversy at the 1999 Academy Awards when Kazan, the legendary director of *On the Waterfront* and *A Streetcar Named Desire*, was given an honorary Oscar for Lifetime Achievement. There were mass protests outside the awards ceremony and letters of disgust to the Academy, sent by actors who had been blacklisted.

'What did he do that was so bad?' I ask.

'He named names. There's nothing lower than that. He was a rat!' hisses the producer, who asks that I don't use his name.

He happens to have a video of the ceremony, along with about 30 others, and he takes some time to put it in the VCR and fast-forward it to the night in question.

'Look at that.' He points to the screen, which shows a huge segment of the audience rise to their feet to applaud Kazan's award. 'At least Steven had the sense to sit down.' He is referring to Steven Spielberg, who is seen applauding politely but refusing to stand. Nick Nolte and Holly Hunter refused to either applaud or stand, but most of Hollywood did indeed get to their feet, including the notorious Hollywood leftie Warren Beatty.

'Shame on them for that display,' the producer says.

When I ask him where I can learn more about the blacklist, he tells me, 'It begins and ends with the Hollywood Ten.'

By the time I learn the story of the Hollywood Ten, I am almost ashamed that my movie is such a frivolous look at Hollywood instead of a documentary about the great injustice this town inflicted on these ten men and so many others, including Will Geer.

The story begins shortly after the Second World War, when the Republican Party took control of the US Congress and helped start an unprecedented reign of terror. The House Un-American Activities Committee (HUAC) declared its intention to investigate whether 'Communist agents had succeeded in implanting Communist messages and values in Hollywood films'. The committee issued a list of potential witnesses, mostly screenwriters but also a number of actors and directors. Ten of these 'unfriendly witnesses' were then summoned to testify before the committee, where they refused outright to answer questions, citing their right to freedom of speech. The question each of them was asked to answer was 'Are you now or have you ever been a member of the Communist Party?' When they refused to answer, these ten writers were formally accused of contempt of Congress. That's where Hollywood's darkest chapter actually begins – not in the actions of the political pond scum who were just following their nature but in the cowardly cave-in that ensued by most of the entertainment industry.

Following a meeting of executives at New York's Waldorf-Astoria Hotel, the Motion Picture Association of America president issued a press release that is today known as the Waldorf Statement. It declared that the ten would be fired or suspended without pay and not re-employed until they were both cleared of contempt charges and had sworn that they were not communists. The Hollywood blacklist was now in effect.

The best-known of the Hollywood Ten was Dalton Trumbo. Unlike many other members of the Hollywood Ten, Trumbo had never been a communist and when he was called before the committee, he was specifically questioned about a script he had written in 1943 called *Tender Comrade* – it was about communal living during wartime, not communist propaganda. He was sentenced to ten months in prison.

On his release, he moved to Mexico with his fellow blacklisted writers Ring Lardner Jr and Albert Maltz, where he continued to work – for fees far smaller than those he'd earned at MGM before the contempt citation. The catch for Hollywood was that he was now writing under assumed names, the pseudonym Ian McLellan Hunter for his 1953 script *Roman Holiday* and, three years later, under Robert Rich, *The Brave One*, both of which won Academy Awards.

In 1970, Trumbo gave a poignant speech to the Screen Writers' Guild about the blacklist, in which he enumerated its effects on a generation: 'The blacklist was a time of evil, and no one on either side who survived it came through untouched by evil. Caught in a situation that had passed beyond the control of mere individuals, each person reacted as his nature, his needs, his convictions and his particular circumstances compelled him to. There was bad faith and good, honesty and dishonesty, courage and cowardice, selflessness and opportunism, wisdom and stupidity, good and bad on both sides.

'When you who are in your 40s or younger, look back with curiosity on that dark time, as I think occasionally you should, it will do no good to search for villains or heroes or saints or devils because there were none; there were only victims. Some suffered less than others, some grew and some diminished, but in the final tally we were all victims because almost without exception each of us felt compelled to say things he did not want to say, to do things that he did not want to do, to deliver and receive wounds he truly did not want to exchange. That is why none of us – right, left or centre – emerged from that long nightmare without sin.'

Among the list of actors who resorted to naming names to save their skins, I was surprised to find Gary Cooper. He starred in my favourite Western of all time, *High Noon*, which is ironically an allegory condemning the Hollywood witch-hunts and those who named names.

I was also intrigued by a story concerning one of the Hollywood figures who refused to name names, the writer Arthur Miller. When Miller was originally called to testify in 1956, his first inclination was to cooperate. But he just happened to be engaged to Marilyn Monroe at the time, who told him, 'Don't give in to those bastards.' And so he refused to cooperate. Ironically, Miller was informed that he could avoid being called to testify if Monroe agreed to be photographed with the chairman of the committee. Monroe refused, but thanks to America's adulation for the movie star, the committee didn't dare jail Miller for his refusal to cooperate. He was instead fined $500 and given a year's suspended sentence. When Monroe's FBI file was declassified years later, it revealed that the Bureau considered her views as 'concisely and positively leftist'. Indeed, even though most people saw Monroe as a brainless blonde bimbo, she was in fact very well read and passionate about social justice, civil rights, feminism and even the environment. This apparently is what attracted her to a left-wing intellectual such as Arthur Miller in the first place.

That day, reflecting on what I had learned about the sad story of the Hollywood blacklist, I couldn't help but think how America has failed to learn any lessons from this tragedy. I still remember in the first few months after 9/11 when a number of reporters, especially radio and TV personalities, were fired for daring to question Bush's handling of the terrorist attacks or straying from the accepted party line.

The most egregious example of this happened to TV talk-show host Bill Maher, whose show, *Politically Incorrect*, I loved to watch. Only six days after 9/11, Maher interviewed a conservative named Dinesh D'Souza, who disputed the widely reported assertion that the terrorists who carried out the attacks were cowards. Instead, she said, these men were 'warriors'.

Maher agreed and went on to say, 'We have been the cowards lobbing cruise missiles from 2,000 miles away. Staying in the aeroplane when it hits the building, say what you want about it, it's not cowardly.'

Maher, of course, did not defend the terrorists or even try to justify their actions; he merely pointed out something which is undeniable. Yet shortly afterwards, ABC TV, bowing to pressure from conservatives, fired him and cancelled his show. He was, in effect, blacklisted from network television from that day forward.

How little things have changed in the American entertainment industry since the days of the Hollywood Ten.

A couple of weeks after my history lesson, I am telling my friend Jill Gold what I learned and she tells me that she has a friend who was blacklisted. Jill is in her early 30s and doesn't spend a lot of time hanging out with geriatric actors and writers, so I wonder how this can be. She offers to introduce me to her friend, who lives in a studio apartment in North Hollywood. When we get there, Lisa invites us in and tells me her story.

'You've heard of the casting couch?' she says. 'Well, it exists, but it doesn't exactly work the way most people think. Maybe in the old days actresses would sleep with producers to get roles, but nowadays it doesn't work like that. It's not the producers who usually choose the talent; it's the casting directors and agencies. It's usually impossible to get to the big producers anyway. In my case, it was a casting assistant for a big agency who straight out implied that I could get a one-time part in a network TV show if I serviced him. From what I hear, it's almost unheard of to actually sleep with somebody on the casting couch. It's all about blow jobs. I had actually done this twice before, once less than two weeks after I arrived in LA from Phoenix. And each time, I got some work as a result. It was totally worth it for me. I couldn't give a shit about the morality; everybody's a whore in this city. Anyway, I blew this casting assistant and I got the part that he promised me, and it was a good credit, so I was happy. But then the guy started calling me and asking me if I wanted to be his 'girlfriend'. I told him I wasn't interested, but he kept promising that I could get a co-starring role in a network show and all kinds of stuff like that. I was tempted for maybe a minute, but the thought of being this guy's sex slave really grossed me out. And it's not like he wasn't cute. He was.

'The second guy I did, last year, was bald and fat. But I guess this is where I drew the line. Actually, I probably would have been OK if it just meant blowing him a couple of times a week, but that's not what he wanted. He literally wanted me to be his girlfriend; he was a bit stalker-ish. He never showed up at my door or anything, but he kept calling. So, finally I tell him that if he doesn't leave me alone, I'll call the head of his agency and tell him what's going on. I had to threaten that twice before he finally left me alone.'

According to Lisa, the guy decided then and there that he would get her blacklisted.

'I can't prove that he did it, but I know he started spreading stories about me around town and definitely at his agency. I wasn't getting any work at all, just a couple of lousy commercials, and I knew that something was wrong. The trouble is I couldn't do anything about it or even disprove the rumours because I didn't know what they were or who he had told what. But I was definitely blacklisted. I still am. I'm probably going to have to move to New York and maybe try to get work on soap operas, but I have no contacts there and it's really, really expensive. It totally sucks!'

I ask her if she's ever heard of the Hollywood Ten.

'Not really,' she replies.

12

★ Tinseltown PI ★

Near the end of my time in Hollywood, there was one subject that everybody was talking about – a subject that alternately riveted and terrified most of the town. It was the case of Hollywood private eye Anthony Pellicano, known as the 'sleuth to the stars', who was indicted along with six associates on over one hundred federal criminal counts of conspiring to wiretap, blackmail and intimidate countless celebrities and business executives, including most notably Sylvester Stallone.

The indictment describes Pellicano as the organiser and leader of the conspiracy that involves a sophisticated web of pay-offs to police, high-tech eavesdropping and similar tactics that read like they come from a Hollywood thriller.

According to the indictment, Pellicano and his clients used the information to secure 'a tactical advantage in litigation by learning their opponents' plans, strategies, perceived strengths and weaknesses, settlement positions and other confidential information'.

'The charges allege a disturbing pattern of criminal conduct in which money flowed freely to encourage sworn law-enforcement officers to violate their oaths to uphold the law and to provide the means for Pellicano and his associates to violate the rights of other individuals,' said US Attorney George Cardona at a news conference the government held to announce the charges.

The 60-page indictment names a slew of alleged high-profile victims 'reasonably expected to conduct their lives without their private information sold for profit, and their private communications intercepted by illegal wiretaps'.

Among the high-profile figures mentioned in the indictment were actors Stallone and Keith Carradine, comedian Gary Shandling and former *Los Angeles Times* reporter Anita Busch, all of whom were allegedly the victims of wiretaps conducted by Pellicano and his associates between August 2000 and November 2002.

'We are not going to stop until we have discovered all of the illegal activities that [Pellicano] participated in,' vowed the FBI official leading the investigation.

Pellicano and two others were charged with violations under racketeering laws usually reserved for Mafia figures. Prosecutors charged them with establishing a criminal 'enterprise' that benefited Pellicano's PI business.

Pellicano pleaded not guilty, but he was being held without bail after a federal prosecutor alleged he was issuing threats from prison against potential witnesses. It was a threat against the *LA Times* reporter, Busch, that led authorities to launch the wiretapping investigation.

In addition, the federal authorities claimed Pellicano and his cronies repeatedly accessed confidential law-enforcement records to gain information against such people as Shandling, former *Saturday Night Live* star Kevin Nealon and countless others.

Pellicano had first appeared on the national radar screen in 1992 when he boasted to *GQ* magazine of the dirty work he had performed for his clients, including blackmail and physical assault. He claimed to have beaten one of his client's enemies with a baseball bat. 'I'm an expert with a knife,' said Pellicano. 'I can shred your face with a knife.'

He had grown up in Al Capone's home town of Cicero, Illinois, and he supposedly had a deep fascination for the Mafia. He even named his son after Don Corleone's assassin in *The Godfather*.

The intrigue all began a few years later when police began investigating death threats that were issued to *LA Times* reporter Anita Busch, who was writing a story about the alleged Mafia ties of actor Steven Seagal.

Another reporter investigating a story on Seagal, *Vanity Fair*'s Ned Zeman, was also a victim of *Godfather*-style tactics while driving through Los Angeles one night, when a Mercedes pulled up menacingly alongside him and the passenger rapped a pistol on the side of Zeman's car. He then pointed it at the terrified reporter, with a one-word message – 'Stop' – then pulled the trigger of the unloaded gun and simply said, 'Bang', before driving off.

On 17 October 2002, an FBI special agent named Stanley Ornellas swore an affidavit in support of a government bid to search the home of an ex-con named Alexander Proctor, who the agent had probable cause to believe was hired by Pellicano to 'burn the car of a *Los Angeles Times* reporter [Busch] who was writing a negative newspaper article about one of Pellicano's celebrity clients [Seagal]'.

According to the affidavit, Proctor told an FBI informant that Seagal had hired him through Pellicano. He allegedly claimed that Pellicano paid him $10,000 to intimidate the reporter. Proctor even left a dead fish, a rose and a note saying 'Stop' on the windshield of Busch's car.

When FBI agents raided Pellicano's office, they discovered fresh military-grade explosives, along with grenades and a pile of cash in the office safe. The amount of explosives found could easily have blown up a car and, according to the agents on the scene, were 'strong enough to bring down an airplane'.

They also found thousands of hours of wiretapped conversations on computer audio files. One of the recordings features the voice of Nicole Kidman, dating from the period of her separation from Tom Cruise in 2001. This discovery led police to question prominent divorce attorney Dennis Wasser, who allegedly enlisted Pellicano's wiretapping services to help orchestrate an amiable split between Cruise and Kidman. Wasser has since been named a 'person of interest' in the investigation, which means he has an open file.

Pellicano served 2½ years in prison for the explosives charges, but now things were getting juicier with the new indictments and speculation abounded throughout Hollywood about what other prominent celebrities might be dragged into the case at trial.

As *Vanity Fair* explained, the repercussions of the scandal in Hollywood would be serious: 'Every divorce, every baby born out of wedlock, every contract dispute, every squabble between studios and talent agencies – involves attorneys, and for the last 20 years when things got nasty, LA lawyers turned to Pellicano, who monitored, investigated, intimidated and in some cases wiretapped their opponents.'

The Hollywood elite were 'scared shitless', according to the article, about the revelations that might come out during the Pellicano trial.

This case actually has a particular resonance for me because I had had my own scary experience a few years earlier with another Hollywood PI who has often been compared to Pellicano – a guy named Jack Palladino. He had also worked for a number of superstars, including Michael Jackson and Snoop Dogg.

It was while I was working on my first book about the death of Kurt Cobain in the late '90s that I had my first encounter with Palladino. It all began with yet another prominent private dick named Tom Grant, who was hired by Courtney Love to find her husband Kurt Cobain after he went missing from an LA rehab centre in April 1994.

After Cobain eventually turned up dead with a shotgun wound in the room above his garage, and the police ruled the death as suicide, Grant continued to work for Courtney for a few months on various things. That is until he levelled the explosive charge that she had lied to him from the beginning and that he was convinced Cobain had been murdered.

But that wasn't all. Grant also claimed he had secretly recorded all his conversations with Courtney as well as with her entertainment attorney, who he said told him she was also suspicious of Kurt's death. The lawyer told Grant on tape that she was convinced that the so-called suicide note found near his body was a 'forgery'.

When I began to investigate these allegations with my writing partner for a magazine article and then a book, to be entitled *Who Killed Kurt Cobain?*, we started to receive a number of very strange phone calls, including a number of threats.

Then one day, as I was arriving home to my Montreal flat, I was greeted by a burly guy, lurking in my courtyard. He introduced himself as an investigator named Jack Palladino who was working for the lawyers of Courtney Love. Could we go to lunch and talk?

Intrigued, I met him, where he produced an enormous file all about my life, including old girlfriends and anything else you might imagine.

'Where did you get all that stuff?' I asked him, amazed.

'I have my methods,' he replied, with a twinkle in his eye, making me wonder at the time whether there was any wiretapping or other illicit methods involved.

He was desperate to read a copy of our manuscript and suggested that he could make it worth my while if I showed it to him. 'I have a lot of connections in the music industry,' he told me, perhaps aware that I was a musician and possibly implying he could get me a recording contract.

It was very obvious what he was really after. He had been hired not by Courtney Love but by her entertainment attorney, who had told Tom Grant she thought Cobain might have been murdered. Palladino was desperate to find out on behalf of his client whether we possessed the tapes where she had allegedly made these remarks, which would have been quite a serious ethical breach if true.

I resisted temptation and refused to show him the manuscript, but Palladino was undeterred. A few months later, I was doing a promotional tour before the launch of my book on Kurt Cobain. Whilst I was appearing on the stage of a Toronto theatre one night, a man suddenly jumped up onstage and started to heckle. It was none other than Palladino, who spent the next half-hour debating with us.

When the event was over, the media gathered around him to ask what he was doing there. He vowed to follow us wherever we spoke in order to set the record straight. At the end of the evening, the MC had announced that our next speaking gig would be two nights later in London. He meant London, Ontario, but Palladino evidently assumed he was actually referring to London, England, because that's where he apparently flew the next day looking for us.

We didn't hear from him again until a few months later when, on the eve of the book's release, he showed up at the office of our New York publisher without an appointment, demanding to see the manuscript. He was unceremoniously thrown out, an incident which was covered by *New York Magazine*.

We later discovered that Palladino and Pellicano had actually once worked for the same celebrity client at the same time – Bill Clinton, when he was running for President in 1992 – and the pair were hired to contain the 'Bimbo eruption' of women who were coming out of the woodwork to claim they had slept with him. In fact, the two PIs may even have worked together on the case.

Ironically, the Cobain private investigator, Tom Grant, who cooperated with our book, happened to be hired by Paula Jones, the Arkansas woman whose sexual harassment suit against Clinton sparked the events that led to his later impeachment. In fact, Grant was instrumental in locating the existence of Monica Lewinsky. At one point, he was even trying to serve a subpoena on Jack Palladino to testify in the Paula Jones case. So this world of celebrity PIs was evidently a small one.

But I never seriously placed Palladino in the same league as somebody like Pellicano and when I got to know him, I even kind of liked the guy. Later, Palladino actually gave an interview to *Vanity Fair* magazine about his old colleague Pellicano in which he said, 'I never took the guy seriously. The way he bragged openly about wiretaps and baseball bats; I mean, I just thought it wasn't real. I didn't understand that his Hollywood clientele lived in that same film-noir world and accepted it as real.'

Ironically, in the middle of the whole Pellicano affair, I conducted an interview with a Hollywood agent for my film who asked me to turn off the cameras and told me he wanted to show me something off the record. He ushered me into a back office and demonstrated the most illicit, sophisticated phone system I had ever seen. He said he had wiretaps hooked up to his clients, his competitor's office down the hall and even his ex-wife, though I'm not sure if I believed him or if he was taking the piss out of me.

'Why do you look so shocked?' he said. 'Everyone does this in Hollywood. You have to tap the actors' phones to make sure they're not cheating on you with other agents and you have to hear what your competitors are up to just in case they get a big lead about a new casting for a film. It's illegal but generally most people do it, thanks to all the high-tech gizmos out there today. Business is tough, so you have to do whatever it takes to get ahead.'

After he told me about his illegal wiretapping practice, I thought to myself I had one of two options: call the FBI, or snitch on him to his competitor. I chose the latter because I wanted to find out if his claim was true.

After leaving his office, I strolled down the hallway and knocked on the door of his competitor, a stocky man in his 60s. I told him what his colleague was up to.

'Where you from?' he asked.

'Canada,' I replied.

'You fucking Canadians are so gullible,' he said. 'If he had taps on me, you think he'd go around advertising it? You think he'd tell a complete stranger? It's like the Mafia – anyone who claims to be in the Mob is definitely not in the Mob. You just don't go around advertising stuff like that.'

Later that day, I asked Hollywood agent Prentice Lennon for his thoughts on what I had heard. 'The guy was definitely pulling your leg,' Lennon said. 'Stuff like that used to go on. But ever since the whole Pellicano scandal, nobody even wants to be caught with a tape recorder in their office.'

13

★ Touting for Tour Business ★

It seems that everywhere I go in Hollywood, in almost every neighbourhood or street corner, there has erupted some scandal or been some tragic death. Likewise everywhere I look in Tinseltown, there is someone advertising a tour to each of these spots – the Dearly Departed tour, the Hollywood Haunted, etc. Most of these tours promise to take visitors to the scenes of notorious Hollywood scandals and share the little-known gory details. They held very little interest for me, though, because most of them focus on recent scandals, such as the cases involving O.J. Simpson, Michael Jackson and Robert Blake. I felt I had already heard enough of the lurid details during the non-stop media barrage during their trials, but it seems that tourists couldn't get enough of that tripe.

However, one day I stumbled upon an ad for a tour revisiting the scandals of Hollywood's golden era. For me, it invoked the Hollywood of film noir that my mother loved – a dark and mysterious era that I always picture in black and white. Maybe a tour would be just the thing to bring that period alive in living colour, so I struck up a deal with the company to take me on a private tour in exchange for being featured in my film.

We set out one morning in a minivan to our first destination: the house where Marilyn Monroe took her last breath in 1962, at 12305 Fifth Helena Drive, Brentwood. I was surprised by how modest the house was, a small bungalow not at all like the opulent mansions one associates with Hollywood celebrities. My tour guide, Mario, knew the case inside out, including, it seemed, every conspiracy theory that has come out since the death.

First, he filled me in on some of the background details. Monroe died on the evening of Saturday, 4 August 1962. According to her housekeeper, Eunice Murray, Monroe had gone to sleep early that evening, but later that night Murray's suspicion was aroused and around 11.30 p.m. she called Marilyn's psychiatrist, Ralph Greenson, who told her to open the bedroom door. When she found the door locked, Murray went to the front of the house to see if she could see anything through the window. There she saw Marilyn lying face down on the bed, apparently unconscious, with empty bottles of pills on her bedside table.

Greenson arrived soon afterwards, broke a window to get in the room and pronounced Marilyn dead. But here's where the first mystery begins. The police weren't actually called until 3.30 a.m., nearly four hours after Marilyn's body was discovered.

The coroner, Thomas Noguchi, 'coroner to the stars', conducted an autopsy and ruled the death was a 'presumed suicide caused by an overdose of barbiturates'. The drug was Seconal, a barbiturate used to treat insomnia and relieve anxiety. Yet it later came out that no Seconal was actually found in Marilyn's stomach or intestines during the autopsy.

Jack Clemmons, who was the first officer on the scene, later claimed that when he entered the home, Eunice Murray was doing laundry and Marilyn's room was very tidy, as though it had been cleaned prior to his arrival. Years later, Clemmons would tell the BBC that he believed the body had been positioned and the scene manipulated. 'It was not a suicide. Marilyn Monroe was murdered and there's no question about it,' he later said.

Even at the time of her death, rumours started almost immediately that there was more to Marilyn's death than the official story. Marilyn famously had an affair with JFK, but when their relationship threatened to derail his presidency John told her it was over, and she then apparently began an affair with his brother, Bobby. That, too, soured and, according to several reports, Bobby broke off with Marilyn shortly before her death, prompting her to threaten to reveal all. Records at the Justice Department, where Bobby worked, revealed that Marilyn had called him eight times during the week of her death. A number of her friends even claimed that she was going to hold a press conference on 6 August to reveal secrets the Kennedys had told her.

Whether or not this is true, we know that Bobby Kennedy visited Marilyn that day, along with his brother-in-law, actor Peter Lawford. Kennedy always denied that he was in Los Angeles that day, but a BBC investigation revealed that Kennedy had taken off that night in a helicopter chartered by Lawford bound for San Francisco.

Lawford's third wife, Deborah Gould, revealed to the BBC that her ex-husband told her Bobby did indeed visit Marilyn that day, to end the relationship between her and the Kennedy brothers.

'Marilyn, from what Peter told me, knew then that it was over . . . And she was very, very distraught and depressed,' Gould revealed. She also said the delay in calling the police after her body was found was to give Kennedy time to get out of town.

Gould also claimed Lawford had told her that he made an 'early-morning sweep' through Marilyn's house after the body was found but before police were called. 'He said he went there, he tidied up the place and did what he could before the reporters found out about the death,' she told the BBC.

That could account for the missing diary, which most likely

contained information about sensitive conversations Marilyn had with the Kennedys, not to mention her affairs, which would have rocked the White House and the country.

Years later, Deputy Coroner Lionel Grandison, who actually signed Marilyn's death certificate, revealed that there had been a 'massive cover-up' by the chief coroner in the case. He claims that evidence was suppressed, the autopsy altered, paperwork taken from the files and that somebody in the department had removed and rewritten key material. And to top it all off, the Monroe police file itself suddenly disappeared.

Besides the Kennedy murder theory, Mario, my guide, tells me, there are a number of other interesting theories involving the Mafia, the heads of the studio, and more plausible theories suggesting Monroe had actually died not of suicide but of an accidental overdose.

I suppose we'll never know the real truth.

Before we leave the house, Mario shares with me another interesting titbit. My old friend Anna Nicole Smith, who had told me so much about her obsession with Marilyn, had actually lived in this very house two years earlier.

It seemed that there were a lot of recurring themes during my time in Hollywood and plenty of weird coincidences. I'm not terribly surprised therefore when Mario announces that the next stop on the tour relates to a notorious scandal involving none other than Charlie Chaplin. From my very first day in LA, when I checked into the Hollywood Roosevelt Hotel and was greeted by a life-size statue of Chaplin in the lobby, to my very first film role, which happened to be a silent movie, the genre Chaplin had made famous, it seemed that the old tramp was stalking me. I had also encountered a woman a couple of months earlier who claimed to have once had a torrid affair with Chaplin.

It had happened one afternoon while I was walking on Hollywood

Boulevard in my His Highness outfit on the way to meet my publicist. Out of the blue, an elderly woman approached me, telling me how much she liked my green shirt. Then she told me she had almost become a movie star back in the early '40s but had run into some 'bad luck'. Learning my lesson from the Ava Gardner incident years back, I decided not to disregard what the woman told me.

She started listing some of the famous actors she had been friends with, including Burt Lancaster, Frank Sinatra and Gene Autry, but the last name she mentioned caught my attention the most – Charlie Chaplin. She told me she was good friends with Chaplin in the early '40s and that they had had a long affair. The woman, who would only give me her first name, Elizabeth, seemed to know everything about the legendary star. When I told her I had acted in a silent film, her response was, 'Wow, he'd be so proud to know that people are still making silent pictures. It's a great art form, all due to the amazing perseverance of Charles. Whatever you do, pretend that there's no camera in front of you and always keep a smile on your face. That was Charles's method to his madness.'

She described Chaplin as a wild guy, someone who was a free spirit. 'If there was a party, he'd be there,' she said. 'He was eccentric, very bold and full of himself. And he loved to be the centre of attention.

'He loved young women and I was only 17 at the time,' she said. 'The fact that I worked as a showgirl turned him on. He loved young women and, as I later found out, he used to have at least a dozen on the go all the time. At one point, he proposed to me, but I knew it was only because I didn't feel like sleeping with him that night. "Charles," I said, "anytime a woman doesn't want to sleep with you, you end up proposing. And then the woman finds out she was the sixth woman you proposed to that day."'

I challenged Elizabeth about the authenticity of her account. She was insulted that I even questioned her story. She told me to meet her at a café called the Coffee Bean later that afternoon. I arrived at the appointed time, but she was nowhere to be found and I assumed I would never see her again. But she walked in a few minutes later, sat down, took a sip from my coffee mug and then pulled out an envelope from her purse containing a short love letter that she said Chaplin once sent her. 'To my sweet, sweet flower, Liz. You make my life worthwhile just by looking at you smile. With love, yours, Charlie.'

Then, she took out a photo of herself, Chaplin and a former actress that I had never heard of named Edna Purviance, who she said was Chaplin's leading lady in most of his films. Actually, I didn't really recognise Chaplin either, because in the photo he looked nothing like the way I had pictured him, since he didn't have his trademark moustache, but when I looked at photos in a Chaplin biography at a bookshop later that day, I realised that it was definitely him.

'Edna and Charlie had a love–hate relationship, but we were all friends,' she told me. 'In fact, Edna became my mentor and guardian angel until the day she died. She protected me from Charles and his friends, telling them that if they abused me, she'd hang them out to dry. She was always concerned about how they always wanted to get me drunk and take advantage of me.'

Elizabeth then went on to describe Chaplin's 'hatred' towards the US government. 'The FBI kept files on him till the day he died,' she said. 'They kept tabs on every move he made. To this day, it's one of the greatest conspiracies of all time,' perhaps exaggerating just a tad. 'He used to cry about it. He could not believe how cowardly these people were, carrying this all on behind his back while he almost single-handedly built America's biggest institution – Hollywood.'

Now, as we visit the house that Chaplin once owned when he was married to Paulette Goddard, Mario describes another side of the silent film legend.

In 1924, the press titan William Randolph Hearst, who was later immortalised in *Citizen Kane*, threw a birthday party on board his yacht, *Oneida*, for Thomas Ince, a powerful Hollywood director/ producer. Among the guests were Chaplin, the gossip columnist Louella Parsons and Hearst's mistress, Marion Davies. The yacht was supposed to sail from San Pedro to San Diego, where the guests would disembark. But midway through the trip, the guest of honour, Ince, was brought ashore in Los Angeles by water taxi. By the next day, he was dead.

Ince's personal physician issued a death certificate, claiming that Ince had died of heart failure. But in the Wednesday's newspapers, blazing headlines announced that Ince had been shot aboard Hearst's yacht. By the afternoon editions, the headlines were gone.

Then stories started circulating about what really happened aboard the yacht that weekend. The most popular involved Chaplin, who Hearst suspected was having an affair with Davies. He had apparently invited them both to the party, hoping to catch them in the act. Sure enough, he caught them in a passionate embrace and pulled a gun. Davies started screaming, which caused Ince to come running in, at which point Hearst accidentally shot him. His intended victim was, in fact, Chaplin.

When the media came enquiring, Chaplin denied even being on the yacht, even though many witnesses placed him there, including Louella Parsons, who was a small-time reporter for one of Hearst's newspapers at the time. But Parsons didn't run the story. Shortly afterwards, she was given a lifetime contract and national syndication in the Hearst chain, which made her one of Hollywood's most powerful and feared figures for decades.

Hearst paid off the mortgage for Ince's wife and provided her with a trust fund, which prompted her to order the immediate cremation of her husband's body before an autopsy could be conducted. And so the mystery went unsolved.

The last stop on our Hollywood scandal tour is the corner of 39th and Norton, where in 1947 the 22-year-old aspiring actress Elizabeth Short was found by a mother and child in an empty lot brutally murdered, six days after she had disappeared from a downtown hotel, sparking the case known as the Black Dahlia. Short always dressed in black and often wore a dahlia flower in her hair, hence the nickname.

Mario brings me to the exact spot where Short's body was found and describes in gruesome detail the scene.

'The body was found literally cut in half,' he says. 'And the blood had been drained from her body. For weeks, the killer taunted police with notes, saying, "Catch me if you can," but they could never catch him. Meanwhile, there were a slew of other similar murders and the media started comparing him to Jack the Ripper. The city and the country were riveted. The Black Dahlia was on the front pages for months, but the crime was never solved.'

The tour had been quite enlightening, even fun. I couldn't help but think that, like everything else, murder and scandal during the golden era were somehow more glamorous than the sex, drug and murder scandals of today.

While mulling this over, I began to think that tourists in Hollywood really shouldn't be wasting their time on such morbid subjects of the past – if they want something to do, I had just the thing: the His Highness Hollywood tour.

One day, I stood on Hollywood Boulevard in normal street clothes with a sign advertising 'Hollywood's First Royal Tour'. I was offering a two-hour guided tour the following day to the 'sights, sounds and glitz' of Hollywood, conducted by a 'member of the royal family'. The fee was only $10, including lunch, a veritable bargain compared with the $35 other tours charged and that didn't even include food. Needless to say, it didn't take me long – less than forty-five minutes, in fact – to sign up seven tourists, which was the capacity of the minivan I planned to rent for the tour.

When the seven lucky tourists show up at the appointed time at the front door of the Hollywood Roosevelt Hotel, His Highness Halperin is there to greet them in his full royal regalia. Two of the seven passengers are Asian and speak very little English. They seem a little bemused at the sight of me. The others are a family of four from Wisconsin – mother, father and two teen kids – and a single woman from Lithuania, who speaks English well but with a strong accent.

'You are about to enjoy the greatest Hollywood experience ever,' I announce to my assembled seven. 'Hop in.'

The first place I take them to is the famous Hollywood sign, which involves a little hike after we park the van. When we get there, I point to the sign and say, 'You see this sign before you? Well, I was sitting in my palace one day a few years ago, looking over my financial statements, and I said to myself, "There has to be more to life than fabulous wealth, women and wine." Then I pictured this legendary sign and it was calling to me. "Come to Hollywood, His Highness," it beckoned, "and share your royal aura with the world." I knew right then and there what I had to do. So I bade farewell to my harem – Rachel, Ruth, Rebekah and Shirley – and I set out to find fame in this city we call Tinseltown.'

One of the kids, who is no older than eleven, looks at me like I'm a freak and says, 'What planet are you from?'

'I hail from planet Earth,' I reply, 'from the Royal Kingdom of Haifa, in the principality of Israel.'

'You're not a king,' she challenges.

'I never said I was,' I reply without hesitation. 'I am Prince Halperin the Third. I do not become King until my father, His Highness Mordecai, passes on to a new kingdom, Heaven.'

'Sure,' she says sceptically, obviously infinitely smarter than the hundreds of people I have already encountered as His Highness who have eaten up my story hook, line and sinker.

'In my kingdom, you can be beheaded for speaking with disrespect to royalty,' I tell her. 'But that's the great thing about America. You can speak your mind. Cherish that freedom, people.'

The next stop on the tour is the condo complex on Bundy Drive where Nicole Simpson was brutally murdered, beginning the world's greatest media circus known as the O.J. Simpson trial. Immediately, I launch into my spiel.

'As you all know,' I bellow, 'I am a Jewish king. I want to tell you the story of another great royal who lived 2,000 years ago. His name was Jesus Christ and, like me, he was a King of the Jews. Well, you all know what happened to him? He was crucified by his enemies.'

I then launch into my Stokely Carmichael voice and point to the house. 'Well, a few years ago another great black man was crucified for a crime that happened right here.'

'Jesus wasn't black,' says the uppity girl.

'According to the great philosopher Malcolm X in his autobiography, Jesus Christ was a black man,' I lecture her. 'The Semites of Palestine were black and that is why he was persecuted. But we aren't talking about the past. We are talking about the present. And in the present, O.J. Simpson is being persecuted for a crime the jury says he didn't commit. He is an innocent man and he needs to be left alone, or the blacks of this nation will rise up and smite their enemies.'

This time, it is the girl's father who interrupts. 'What the hell are you talking about? Everybody in this country except 12 brainless idiots knows he did it. You're not asking us to believe that you think O.J. is really innocent?'

'It is your justice system, not mine,' I reply. 'In my country, we would have roasted O.J.'s testicles and served them in our Passover soup, but the American justice system says he is innocent and I have to stand by the brother and protest his crucifixion.'

The father actually chuckles at this, and I see some recognition in his face that he is having his leg pulled. Lucky thing, because I swear that another few minutes of this and he could have yanked his family away, even though we are in the middle of nowhere in a ritzy residential district with no cabs to be found for miles.

'Who's ready for lunch?' I suddenly ask. I had promised them a free lunch as part of the tour so we head for the only establishment that I can afford on the measly $10 that each of them had paid, a Taco Bell. The van itself had cost me almost $200, so I was already taking a financial bath on this tour. If they think they are in for some fine dining, they are to be disappointed. However, I decide to make the lunch a little more palatable for them.

'In my country, this is the food of kings,' I inform them, pointing to my burrito. 'My father and his harem eat nothing but burritos and enchiladas. It is said to keep one's blood blue.'

By this time, the jig is up with the Wisconsin family, who laugh at nearly everything I say. But the Asian couple and the Lithuanian woman just stare at me with a befuddled look on their faces.

After lunch, I take them to the last stop on the tour, the Hollywood Wax Museum on Hollywood Boulevard, not far from where the tour had begun. Here, wax figures of all the Hollywood greats are displayed. My group all seem happy that they are finally going to see something of substance, but tickets are something like $15, more than they had all paid for the entire tour, and there is no way I intend to shell out even more of my dough. Instead, I have something else in mind.

I pass out a sheet and a pen to each of the seven people and tell them it's time for them to help 'crusade for justice'. On the page is a petition calling for the wax museum to display a wax figure of His Highness Halperin, alongside the existing figure of Princess Grace, to recognise the important contribution of Hollywood's 'second great royal personality'. (YouTube)

For some reason, my group doesn't get into the spirit of

the occasion and not one of them makes any attempt to obtain signatures. I obtain a grand total of two signatures myself, from a couple of twenty-something female tourists, one of whom tells me, 'If that doesn't work, I'll be glad to drip hot wax all over your body.'

By this stage, I have already lost the Wisconsin family, who have paid for admittance to the museum. Soon afterwards, the tour complete, I drop the other three off in front of Grauman's Chinese Theater, the famous Hollywood landmark where the footprints of the great movie stars are immortalised in cement.

None of them can say they didn't get their money's worth.

14

★ Barbra Streisand, My Idol ★

I am wrapping up my documentary in Los Angeles in December 2005 when news comes from the US Supreme Court that the appeal of former LA gang member Tookie Williams has been rejected and the way is now clear for his execution.

The Williams case had actually become something of a cause célèbre during my time in LA. Williams, who was black, was one of the founders of the notorious gang the Crips, long-time rivals of the Bloods, with whom they have intensely fought for street supremacy, leaving countless dead bodies in their wake. In 1979, Williams was arrested for the murders of four people during an armed robbery and was sentenced to death, marking the beginning of a long stay on death row while he wound his way through the appeals process.

In 1993, Williams had suddenly announced that he was a changed man. He renounced his old behaviour, became a committed anti-gang activist and apologised for founding the Crips. He even wrote seven children's books while he was in prison and did appear to have genuinely changed.

My favourite story about Williams is his being given a President's Call to Service Award for his good deeds. He received a letter from President George W. Bush congratulating him for showing 'the outstanding character of America'. A few days later, after uproar in the media, a Bush spokesman declared the President had no way of knowing that the person he was honouring was a condemned multiple murderer.

When the day finally comes for Williams' execution, scheduled for midnight, LA is in chaos. Celebrities and activists are holding a vigil outside the prison and hundreds of thousands of people have signed petitions urging Governor Schwarzenegger to grant Williams clemency. Public officials are worried that the city's black community will erupt if the execution takes place, much like it did during the infamous Rodney King riots over a decade earlier.

Perhaps it's a feeling of *noblesse oblige*, or the queasy feeling I always get in my stomach about race in America, but I sense it is up to His Highness to do something about the situation, so I put on my outfit and bring a soapbox to the corner of Hollywood and Vine, the famous Los Angeles intersection. Not that I support Tookie, but I believe in redemption and it's clear that Williams is worth more to society alive than dead.

So I get on my soapbox and start preaching to passers-by that LA will go up in flames if they fry Tookie. 'Get on your cells and yell before this town goes to hell when they fry Tookie's bell,' I shout.

To anybody who stops I give the number of Schwarzenegger's office, imploring people to protest the execution. When a man finally asks me who I am, I tell him I was sent by Dr Louis Farrakhan, the militant leader of the black radical group, the Nation of Islam, and Ross Perot, the former US presidential candidate. I tell the crowd that Farrakhan had appointed me the first white member of the Nation of Islam because of my royal descent. I inform my audience that Farrakhan and Perot have united to form a new group called 'Blacks Against Whites, Whites Against Blacks'. I ask the assembled crowd, now numbering about 75, how many think Tookie should be fried. About 60 raise their hands. Then, in my best Stokely

Carmichael voice, I start preaching to the crowd. I rant and rave like my old idol, the Black Panther leader whom I had befriended in 1985, when I brought him to Montreal to speak on a human-rights lecture series I organised in university. 'You've got to free Tookie from the perpetrator of injustice, from Satan and the Son of Sam, so Tookie can eat a cookie and be free.' The pro-execution Tookie crowd actually applaud at the end of my ten-minute speech. Then I take questions from the crowd. Only one person is belligerent towards me, calling me an accomplice to murder.

Still upset about Tookie's execution, which happened on schedule that evening, and the overwhelming support it received from the public at large, I decide to take matters into my own hands. I want to see just how racist Hollywood is. I can't help wonder whether a white murderer who repented like Tookie would have aroused the same bloodlust that I witnessed. And isn't this the town that right-wing Americans always cite as a bastion of bleeding-heart liberalism? I certainly haven't witnessed that to date. Then I think of how few black actors, let alone Hispanics and other ethnic minorities, have received Oscars over the years, and how blacks in films are still overwhelmingly portrayed as criminals, pimps and thugs.

So, I decide to spend one day on Hollywood Boulevard as a white film director seeking funding for my next film and the next day dressed up as a black film director. The spiel will be exactly the same: I'm an aspiring film director trying to raise money to shoot my next film. The storyline, naturally, will be that it's about a young member of the royal family who falls out with his queen because he admits he's gay and decides to pursue his real dream of becoming an actor in Hollywood.

I dress up both days in the same outfit – an LA Dodgers baseball cap, blue jeans, a Fubu T-shirt and a pair of black army boots I bought at a second-hand store for $9 in downtown LA. The only difference will be on day two I'll hire a make-up artist to make me look black.

My inspiration for this scheme is a book I read as a teenager called *Black Like Me*. The author, John Howard Griffin, a white man, took a special supplement that darkened his skin in order to see how society treated blacks. The results shocked him and his readers, and his story had a powerful impact on me growing up. Now, more than four decades later, I assumed American society had undergone a dramatic shift in race relations. But had it?

The first day, as a white director, is a success. People stop to talk to me and are very interested in helping me out. I only take written commitments for cash. I hold a clipboard with a pledge sheet I designed at Kinkos. (Kinkos had become very handy in my undercover pursuits – first getting me on the red carpet and now helping me raise the dough for my next 'film'.) By the end of the day, I have collected over 800 signatures, raised more than $2,000 in pledges from potential investors (I refuse to take cash because I don't want to be arrested for fraud), received two phone numbers from people who say they work in the industry and can help me out and I even get myself a free lunch at a sushi bar when the owner passes by and says, 'I won't invest in your film, but lunch is on me if you give out my restaurant's business card to everyone who stops to talk to you.' For a free lunch, why not? So to everyone who comes by, I slip his card.

Nobody even gives me a hint of negative vibes while I'm dressed as a white director.

The next day is the complete opposite. I arrange to have my disguise put on by a local LA make-up artist named Maddy Harris at 8 a.m. It takes Maddy the better part of three hours to make my face and hands look black. She covers me with foundation, dark make-up and touch-ups. By the end of the session, she exclaims, 'You look blacker than Snoop Dogg!' Actually, I'm thinking I look more Latino than black, and she's a white girl, so what does she know?

Next, Maddy puts in a couple of hair extension braids to make me look more legit. 'Wow,' she says. 'No one would ever know you're white.' Then I put on the black Afro wig I have rented beneath my LA Dodgers cap and I'm ready to go.

I take a cab back to the same spot in front of the Kodak Theater on Hollywood Boulevard. The cab driver is my first test. I'm worried he'll think I'm early for Halloween. When I get in, the driver, who's black, says, 'Yo, bro, what's up? Where you off to today?' I respond in my Stokely Carmichael voice. 'Yeah, brother, it looks nice out today. Let's touch down at the Kodak Theater. I have some business there.' Then the driver says to me, 'You look familiar, brother. Are you an actor?' I respond, 'No, I'm a director and I'm off to promote my new film at the Kodak.'

'Are any of your films well known?' he asks.

'Not yet, brother, but they should be. You know how this town is, they don't like the brothers too much here, especially when they want to make it behind the scenes.'

I struck gold. He lashes back: 'Tell me about it, man. I used to be an actor and all them motherfuckers wanted me to play was jungle parts or to be a comedian. They only want us to look like monkeys on the screen. That's why I drive this cab, because I refuse to play their game.' When we arrive, I give him $12, which includes a $4 tip. He gives me the black handshake before I get out.

I seem to have passed my first test with flying 'colours'.

The day is an absolute disaster. Dressed exactly the same as I was 24 hours earlier, I am about to have the most harrowing experience of my undercover pursuit. At the end of the first two hours, I have collected only four signatures, have not raised a dime in pledges and have been called pretty much every name in the book. The worst is one guy from Long Beach who tells me he's in the business as an assistant director. 'You look more like a thug than a film director,' he says. 'What gangsta movie are you making?' When I try to tell him what I am really doing, he says, 'Maybe you should go to Harlem to make your film. Try raising your money on those streets – not here. Please don't cheapen the sidewalk of the stars here.'

One woman comes up to me and says, 'Aren't you too proud to beg? Go get a real job.' I give her the finger and a minute later she comes back with her goon of a boyfriend, who threatens to 'kick the shit out of me' if I do not apologise.

'I ain't apologising to anyone who calls me a beggar,' I say, aware that he's not about to assault me on a busy intersection in the heart of Hollywood, especially with my black cameraman close by. 'You're not worth my time, nigger. Go back to the jungle.'

The day is turning nasty. Not only are the whites hostile but the black passers-by are not exactly loosening their purse strings either. Finally, the day comes to an end three and a half hours after I began with a total of eight signatures and no pledges when two cops come up to me and threaten to arrest me if I don't move on. 'No soliciting here,' the cops say. 'Move on or else we'll take you in.'

The day before, standing as a white man for hours in the exact same spot, I never heard a peep out of the cops, even though I must have seen at least ten throughout the day. Less than 24 hours later, standing as a black man, I receive a civics lesson about the real America.

Unfortunately, I have a lot of trouble removing the make-up. Maddy had warned me it might take some time to get it off, but I had no idea I'd spend the next four days walking around Hollywood looking like what one friend called 'a cross between Richard Pryor burning his skin off free-basing and Michael Jackson going without a week of treatment to whiten his skin'. Here I am, supposed to be going out to auditions, but how can I show my face looking like this? The casting directors will probably call the cops the moment I walk in the door.

- ★ -

The whole time I was in LA, during six different trips over three years, I stayed at the Hollywood Roosevelt. One night, there was a sign announcing a VIP reception being held in the lobby in honour of the American Film Institute.

When I go down to check it out, I practically bump into Bruce Willis, who is attending the reception. I immediately decide I will try to get in, so I race back upstairs, put on my His Highness outfit and sashay back. In the cordoned-off area eating a canapé, I see Jack Valenti, president of the Academy of Motion Pictures Arts and Sciences, who gives a boring spiel at the Oscars every year about the Academy. I call him over and introduce myself, telling him my grandfather, the prince, had designed the Blossom Room at the Roosevelt where the first Oscar ceremony was held.

'I'd love to chat with you about some of the Oscar stories he told me about that first ceremony,' I tell him, hoping he will invite me into the party.

But he's not buying it. Maybe if I had been dressed normally it would have worked. He says, 'You're pulling my leg, son. Who the hell are you for real?' (I later find out that the first ceremony lasted only five minutes with thirteen awards handed out, so there probably weren't a lot of anecdotes to be had.) Within 30 seconds, I am escorted out of the area by security. They cannot eject me from the hotel because I am a registered guest there, so security tells me to stay at least 20 yards away from where the party is taking place. When Valenti walks by again and looks over, I stick my tongue out at him, letting him know there is nothing he can do. He promptly gives me the finger. Not very dignified for somebody in his position, I think to myself.

Another day, an artist friend of mine tells me her parents live in the same condo complex as Ringo Starr. I am determined to meet him. It is only fitting, after all, that His Highness Halperin should pay a visit to the local rock and roll royalty. I had already met one

Beatle a couple of years earlier, when I was hired to perform with my band at the Montreal Grand Prix. George Harrison was in town to see the race and over drinks I proposed writing an authorised biography. He seemed very open to the idea and asked to read some of my previous books. The details were still being worked out at the time of his death in 2001. I was all set to move forward with the book anyway when his wife threatened a lawsuit because she was planning to revise and re-release a biography she had written years earlier. She wouldn't have had a leg to stand on, my agent told me, but I couldn't afford a potentially costly legal battle, so I backed off.

Anyway, I hang around the complex for two days with my friend, swimming at the pool, until I see Ringo strolling on the grounds with his wife, Barbara Bach. I casually walk up to him and with a straight face ask him if the Beatles will ever reunite. It was clearly a joke that I stole from an old *Saturday Night Live* routine, based on the fact that each Beatle had been asked this question a million times following the break-up of the group in 1970. But to my amazement, he replies, 'Maybe.' I'm not sure what Ringo's smoking these days, but two of the Fab Four are dead, so perhaps a reunion is a little late. Maybe he meant himself and Paul onstage, with John and George added in virtually, something like Celine Dion's recent embarrassing duet with Elvis Presley on *American Idol*.

Speaking of *American Idol*, I actually ran into Simon Cowell one morning on Hollywood Boulevard, coming out of a Banana Republic store. I approached him and asked him if he thought I could pass for royalty. He smiled and gave me a thumbs-up. He seemed considerably more laid-back – and much nicer – than he does on the show. In fact, I noticed that seconds later he gave a homeless man some cash, and even took a minute to chat with him, something I suspect most celebrities rarely do.

The most genuine of all the celebrities I meet while filming, however, is the late-night talk-show host Jay Leno, who is a friend of Vincent Chase. I was planning to do a little schtick with Jay, demanding he book His Highness as a guest on the *Tonight Show*, but when I meet him as he is heading to tape his show, he seems so down to earth, friendly and sincere that I don't have the heart. Instead, I confide in him the nature of my documentary and ask him whether he thinks Hollywood deserves to be exposed.

'It's funny,' he replies. 'I'm not the best judge of Hollywood's true nature. I've met just about every big name in the business, but they're all very nice to me because my show is so powerful, so I really haven't experienced the back-stabbing and viciousness that everybody always talks about. Now, if you want to ask me about the comedy circuit, that's another story.'

Back in Montreal, already editing my film, I have all but given up on the idea of landing a film role or of having my documentary aired. Then I receive news.

My agent calls to tell me that the casting director for a network TV mini-series about Ronald Reagan had seen my head-shot and thinks I have a 'terrific look'. The film is being shot in my home town, Montreal. I had actually heard a lot of buzz already about this movie, which was to be titled *The Reagans*. An enormous controversy had erupted when CBS had announced the project because of the actor who had been cast to play Reagan: James Brolin.

The American hard-right was furious, not because they had anything against Brolin himself but because he happened to be married to Barbra Streisand, public enemy number one to US Republicans since she is passionate and outspoken in her liberal views. They were convinced that the association with Streisand meant that the movie would be a hatchet job designed to tarnish the reputation of their beloved Reagan.

Now, to be fair, it can no longer be said that Reagan is the dumbest

President in American history, a fact that many liked to toss around in the '80s when old mush for brains was wreaking havoc. No, the current occupant of the White House makes Reagan look like a Rhodes scholar; sometimes I yearn nostalgically for the days when he and Maggie still ruled the world, mere amateurs in the art of bloodshed compared to their ideological successors, Dubya and Blair.

I immediately start mulling over what part I will be playing in the film. My preference is for a Doctor Strangelove-like presidential adviser, making crank calls to the Kremlin on the red phone while Ronnie is off in a corner of the Oval Office playing with his toy train set.

'Hello, Brezhnev, is your refrigerator running?'

'Why, yes, Mr President, why do you ask?'

'Well, you better go catch it.'

When I report to the set, however, I am informed that I am to play a lowly stunt man.

'I've never done stunt work,' I tell the casting director's assistant, envisioning a scene where I accidentally get sodomised by a monkey while recreating Reagan's most famous film role, *Bedtime for Bonzo*.

'It doesn't matter. We want you. You're going to be in one of the best scenes,' she replies.

It turns out I will be playing a cowboy, which is actually kind of cool. It takes me back to my childhood, playing cowboys and Indians with my brother and sister.

The day before the shoot, I am sent to a warehouse in the east end of Montreal to be fitted out in cowboy duds. They have trouble finding me the right cowboy boots because I have size 12 feet. Finally, after sifting through dozens of pairs, they find me the right size.

'You have the biggest feet out of any cowboy here, clown feet,' says the wardrobe guy. 'You know what they say about actors with big feet?'

'No, what do they say?' I ask him.

'Big feet, big cheat. Actors with big feet get all the girls and cheat on their girlfriends.'

I look at him as if he is nuts, which he probably is.

When I arrive on set for my scene, they send me right to the dressing-room, which I share with a slew of others. On my way, I bump into James Brolin, who is nice enough to shake my hand and welcome me.

In my contract, it's specified that no cameras of any kind are allowed on set and if anyone gets caught, they will be automatically fired. I had ignored this rule and brought a digital camera into my dressing-room, where I try to take pictures and video of myself dressed in cowboy attire to use for my own film. While I'm clicking away, another stunt man walks in and catches me.

'Are you crazy?' he says. 'If anyone catches you doing this, you'll get thrown off the set.'

Two minutes later, he is holding the door closed, with his body against it, taking photos of me with my camera. I tell him I'm doing an undercover exposé and he tells me, 'It's about time someone exposed these assholes. I've been in this business for 20 years now and the people totally suck. They're selfish, greedy and inhumane.'

Sensing some juicy gossip, I ask him for examples.

'I've worked with local crews here forever and have never received a birthday card, not even a Christmas card.'

I'm thinking why would anybody from a major production send a Christmas card to a mere stunt man? This business sure produces a lot of neurotic whiners.

After I get dressed in my outfit, one of the assistant directors starts giving me advice on how to act in the scene. It's a saloon scene from Reagan's old '50s TV Western and I'm supposed to trip right over Brolin. The scene is no longer than 30 seconds. Brolin's in a corner memorising his lines. He has them written out on a small piece of paper in his pocket. I presumptuously ask if he wants me to read him through his lines, but he says he is OK. He is the spitting image of Ronald Reagan. It's a little bit eerie.

The film's director, Robert Allan Ackerman, is wearing a black shirt with a picture of a naked woman on the back. I can't help but think how Reagan would have disapproved; Nancy would have thrown a shit fit.

Six other guys are also on set with us, dressed as cowboys as well, drinking at the saloon bar. After I trip over Brolin, he goes up to one of the cowboys and punches him out, resulting in a good old-fashioned barroom brawl. It's a tricky scene to get right. After the first take, the director tells me, 'Good job.' He then turns to everyone else and says the same thing. He takes Brolin aside and gives him some advice. We do two more takes and Ackerman gives us a ten-minute break. During this time, I get a chance to talk to Brolin.

I had overheard him earlier saying that he's interested in sending his daughter to McGill University in Montreal, possibly in the music programme, so I tell him how good the McGill programme is, especially their big-band curriculum. He starts quizzing me about it, even though I tell him I actually attended the Concordia music programme, not McGill's. Before the conversation is over, I tell him how impressed I am with his resemblance to Reagan.

'I may not have agreed with everything he stood for – well, anything he stood for, really – but he certainly was one of a kind,' Brolin says. 'I'm actually excited to be doing this role because it's very challenging to play a man whose politics were so abhorrent to me.'

After a few more takes, union rules call for a lunch break. The actors tell me at lunch how impressed they are with the lunch that day. 'Usually it's low budget, except for the stars,' one actor tells me. 'But because we're such a small group today, it's gourmet for all.

This is great.' We chow down on salmon, shrimp, pasta and salads. Everything is cooked perfectly.

Before the end of lunch, I notice a familiar nose. I do a double-take. The woman in sunglasses chatting with Brolin is none other than Barbra Streisand. Later, a lighting technician tells me she had driven down from New York two days earlier in an SUV because she hates to fly. No one else seems to recognise her. Most of the other cowboys on set are French-speaking Montrealers.

I can't believe I'm this close to Streisand, who I consider one of the most talented people on earth. This is a woman who has won two Oscars, countless Grammy and Emmy awards and has a voice like butter. When I was eight years old, I sat through three consecutive showings of her movie *What's Up, Doc?*, laughing for hours at her comic genius. Now here she is, just a few feet away. A few years earlier, I had written the very first biography of Celine Dion, whose voice is often compared to that of Barbra; indeed, as far as vocal range goes, Dion and Mariah Carey can definitely hold their own with Streisand. But neither has any soul, which is what puts Barbra in a league of her own. Jewish soul.

But what really sets Streisand apart for me is her political courage. For decades, she has fought the good fight, battling for social justice and speaking out against the devastating misery inflicted by Republican Party policies. Her political blog at barbrastreisand.com is the best compendium of accessible information about the lies of Bush and his cronies, and their dishonesty over the Iraq war, that I've ever come across. This is why the American right is so apoplectic over her indirect association with the Reagan project, sensing the imminent celluloid skewering of their hero.

I finally summon up the nerve to go up to her and tell her I am a huge fan of hers, but not President Reagan. 'I was never exactly his best friend either,' she tells me. 'In fact, we did a lot of thinking before getting on board this project.'

She explains that Brolin was reluctant at first to play the role until he read the script and discovered that it offered a 'balanced' portrayal.

Streisand apparently doesn't drink coffee, which, along with water, is the only drink available at the Craft services table, so she asks if somebody can get her a cup of tea. 'Earl Grey, if you have it,' she yells to nobody in particular. A woman with a clipboard says she'll get it. Sensing an opportunity to bond with Yentl herself, I say to the crew woman, 'I'll have a cup too, please.'

She chats with Brolin until the tea comes about ten minutes later, and I try to eavesdrop unobtrusively, but I can't catch much of their conversation. Finally, the tea arrives in Styrofoam cups, and Streisand pours hers into a plastic mug she takes out of her bag. I say to her, 'The only place anybody ever offers you tea any more is England.'

'Not any more,' she says. 'When I first went there, everybody drank tea, but now it's just the old-timers. Everybody drinks coffee now. I was once invited for "tea" at a house in Hampstead and what do you think they served? Coffee.'

I tell her a story about my old British landlady, Betty Hawkins, who had cared for Judy Garland, an old friend of Streisand.

'It's just terrible what happened to her,' she says, nodding her head sadly. 'I loved Judy. She actually gave me a lot of advice when I was just coming up about how to avoid all the crap and what she called the "bad guys". It's too bad she didn't take her own advice. I was never actually a victim of the casting couch; I guess I was lucky, but it's still used all the time in Hollywood and New York. You be careful.'

At some point in the conversation, it registers with me that I'm actually having a casual conversation with Barbra Streisand, one of the most famous people in the world. It seems a little surreal.

By the time shooting resumes in the afternoon, Streisand is right there, front and centre. Before the cameras start rolling, she tells a Reagan joke that has the cast and crew laughing. 'The first time I met Ronald and Nancy Reagan,' she says, 'he actually sounded somewhat intelligent. Then I realised that I could see Nancy's lips moving, so I asked her if she could repeat that trick while drinking a glass of water.'

After one more take, Streisand makes a suggestion for how the scene can be simplified and improved. Before you know it, she has taken over and we are being directed by one of the greatest legends in show-business history. Ackerman seems in awe of her and is quite content to let her take the reins.

Indeed, the scene seems to flow a lot better with her improvements. Suddenly, instead of tripping over Brolin, which always seemed unnatural, Streisand tells me to walk around him. The fight scene also becomes much less chaotic.

Nevertheless, she is never entirely satisfied and keeps telling Ackerman to have us do it 'just one more time'. I had read that Streisand could be a bit of a diva, but I can see no sign of it. She treats the crew, and even us lowly stunt people, with complete respect.

And the best part of it all: because of Barbra's direction, we get paid double overtime as the shoot goes on much longer than expected. My rent is paid for the next couple of months thanks to her. And, before I leave, Brolin thanks me for my advice about McGill and even tells me that if I'm ever in Malibu, I should look them up. As if that's going to happen – he conspicuously failed to give me a phone number or an address. Still, it's a nice gesture.

This is my only scene, but before filming is completed a few weeks later a fresh brouhaha ensues when the script is leaked to the media and the US right-wing forces rear their ugly heads once again.

In one scene in the leaked script, the film's Nancy Reagan advises her husband that the federal government should take steps to deal with AIDS. In the film, Reagan is portrayed as saying:

'They that live in sin shall die in sin.' There is no actual source for such a quote and the scriptwriter admits she invented the line. Of course, such creative licence is taken all the time with biopics. And the facts speak for themselves. When the AIDS epidemic first started to spread and immediate action was urged by scientists to address the issue, Reagan bowed to the powerful Christian right and repeatedly refused to commit federal research money to combat the new plague. After all, they reasoned, it was only gays who were dying of the disease and it served them right for their sins. As a result of Reagan's stalling – which was particularly shameful because some of his own advisers and a number of his former Hollywood friends had contracted AIDS – millions ended up dying needlessly.

Of course, the accusations started flying fast and furiously that it was Streisand, Reagan's ideological enemy, who was responsible for the hatchet job. She immediately denied it, claiming she had absolutely nothing to do with the project, which, as I knew, wasn't entirely true.

Nevertheless, these and other creative liberties in the script provided the right with enough ammunition and they successfully forced CBS to cancel its plans to air the mini-series, shuffling it off instead to its cable outlet, Showtime, where it was guaranteed low ratings and millions fewer viewers. In announcing its decision, CBS admitted the programme did not present a 'balanced portrayal'.

When CBS announced its decision, Streisand issued a statement that the move was a 'sad day for artistic freedom. This was an organised Republican spin machine at work. This is censorship, pure and simple.'

On her website, she wrote, 'I am deeply disappointed that CBS, the network that in 1964 gave me complete artistic control in creating television specials, has now caved in to right-wing Republican pressure to cancel the network broadcast of the movie *The Reagans*.

(And I say MOVIE – because this is NOT a documentary – it's a television drama.)'

I was just as pissed off as Barbra because my mass-market entertainment debut had been relegated to the dustbin of TV history. But that's showbiz.

A few weeks later, I get another call from my agent telling me she has some more work for me, this time in an NBC pilot called *EDNY*, starring Billy Baldwin. As it turns out, I am nothing more than a glorified extra, though I am featured quite prominently in one police-precinct scene where I stand by Baldwin's side. I have a chance to talk to him a little between takes and even manage to sneak a small camera on set with which I snap some photos. I asked Baldwin if he thinks this show has a chance of being picked up by the network.

'Of course, otherwise I wouldn't be wasting my time. I think it could do great.'

From what I had witnessed, the prospect seemed unlikely. The script was god-awful and the whole premise was stiff. Sure enough, when the network announced its autumn schedule a couple of months later, *EDNY* was nowhere to be found.

In April 2007, I was in New York meeting with potential distributors of my completed documentary when I stopped into a Starbucks on 8th Avenue for coffee. There, sitting at a corner table, was Billy Baldwin with his more famous brother, Alec, drinking a cup of coffee. I went up to Billy, said hello and reminded him I had worked with him on *EDNY*. I also chatted with Alec, who by that time I had also worked with, but that's another story.

I had read various tabloid accounts of his messy six-year battle with his ex-wife, Kim Basinger, over custody of their daughter, but if that was bothering him on this day, he certainly didn't show it.

Three days after my encounter with the Baldwins, celebrity site TMZ.com obtained a leaked copy of a voicemail message that Alec had left for his 11-year-old daughter, Ireland, after she had failed to answer her father's scheduled morning phone call from New York. On the voicemail, Alec goes berserk, saying, 'Once again, I have made an ass of myself trying to get to a phone. You have insulted me for the last time. I don't give a damn that you're 12 years old or 11 years old or a child, or that your mother is a thoughtless pain in the ass who doesn't care about what you do. You've made me feel like shit. I'm going to straighten your ass out. This crap you pull on me with this goddamn phone situation that you would never dream of doing to your mother, and you do it to me constantly over and over again. You better be ready Friday the 20th to meet with me.'

He later issued a teary apology and insisted that his fans have no idea of the hell he had been through over the past several years as a father fighting for custody. He also announced his intention to quit acting so he can publicise the issue of 'parental alienation'.

When I'd talked to him briefly a few days earlier, he'd looked and sounded as if he didn't have a care in the world. It just goes to show that you never know what's really going on behind the closed doors of these celebrities' opulent mansions.

While I was in New York that week, I had a chance encounter with one of my two favourite celebs of all time – one being the late trumpet great Louis Armstrong and the other talk-show diva Oprah Winfrey. I met Oprah while strolling in Central Park with my five-year-old daughter, Clover. Oprah, wearing a tracksuit and with an entourage of four people, who I assumed were bodyguards, was taking a break from jogging and getting ready to cross the street near Columbus Circle to leave the park. I had no idea I was next to her until some homeless-looking guy said, 'You're standing next to Oprah.' I could not believe it. She was wearing sunglasses, so I had to look closely, but there was no mistaking those features. There she was, looking beautiful and fit. I was actually a little tongue-tied, but I told her she looked much sexier in person than on TV. Oprah gave a smile. After I asked, she graciously lifted Clover so I could take several pics of them together. Thank God I had my digital camera on me. Unfortunately, I blew the best photo opportunity of all time by getting star-struck and forgetting to get myself in the picture.

Ironically, this was the second time I had struck out with Oprah. In early September 2001, one of her producers called to get me on her show to discuss my undercover book about models, which she said they had read and liked. A few days later, 9/11 happened and Oprah spent the next several months covering it, canning all her scheduled guests during that time and ruining my chance at an automatic million seller. Damn that Bin Laden!

Back in LA, I wake up one morning with a scheme to hitchhike around Hollywood for one full day to see what kind of characters will pick me up dressed as His Highness. I hold out a sign, 'Give a Ride to a Royal', and ask each driver to take me to the nearest kosher restaurant, claiming that I am craving food that I am allowed to eat. I tell them I'm a Jewish king and say that I am having a tough time finding kosher food in LA. I never have to wait more than five minutes to get a ride. Surprisingly, seven out of the nine people who pick me up that day are women driving alone. They are completely nuts. What woman in her right mind would pick up a freak like me, a total stranger who looks like a nutcase, dressed up to the nines on a sweltering 92-degree day, and risk ending up having her body found the next day in a ditch or dismembered?

Virtually everyone who picks me up is involved in the entertainment industry in some way. This does not surprise me at all, because it seems that everyone you meet in Tinseltown, from the person pumping gas to the drive-in cashier at McDonald's, is trying to make it to the big time.

The first person to pick me up is Rhoda, a southern belle from Charleston, who has been in LA for six months trying to find an agent and going to auditions. Rhoda tells me she has never picked up a hitchhiker before. I asked her why she chose me and she said because she had a good feeling about me when she saw my garb and my sign. It turns out she knows a great kosher restaurant.

What a whack job, I think to myself, seated in the passenger seat of a 1992 Toyota Corolla that makes Fred Flinstone's old stone car look like a Jaguar. Rhoda starts peppering me with questions about my royal lineage. She is so impressed that at one point she calls her mother and puts me on the phone with her. She tells me it will make her mother's day because her mother loves the queens of both England and Denmark (does Denmark even have a queen?) and has always dreamt of actually talking to a member of a royal family first-hand. Who would believe that a guy hitchhiking in Hollywood is a member of a royal family? She drops me off at Cantor's Restaurant on Fairfax and tells me I'll find kosher food inside. When I tell her I've forgotten my credit card, she takes out a fistful of $5 and $1 bills and tells me to go 'feast on them kosher eats your Jewish people fill their tummies with'. Of course, I politely refuse her handout.

The next person to pick me up is a 33-year-old wannabe film director named Matt who is down and out, trying to make it and considering changing his life by becoming a priest. He has just about given up on his dream, but I tell him to never give up. He asks me for advice on what to do – I tell him to find himself.

He tells me he even considered becoming a Jew at one point. 'Everybody in this town is Jewish, so I thought maybe the best way to network is to hunt the Jews down at the synagogue.' Wow, I think to myself, as if my people don't have enough nutcases out there hunting us down.

I tell Matt to forget about finding me some kosher food – I have a place in mind that might help him change his life. I make him drive to the Scientology Center on Hollywood Boulevard. Let him 'hunt' them down. Leave the Jews alone.

I tell him Scientology changed my life forever and that it might do the same for him. 'Forget the priesthood. Go in there and meet your maker,' I say. Yeah, I think to myself, this guy's maker should really be a shrink in Beverly Hills who tells him to go back home to Chicago and find a real job.

There are several other uneventful encounters, but the strangest ride I get that day is on the back of a Harley-Davidson. Louise, 19, is trying to make it as an actor and claims she has a rich sugar daddy in Hollywood, a top-level producer, who takes care of her.

'He's married with kids, so he doesn't take up a lot of my time,' she boasts. 'All he expects from me is to be with him a couple of hours a week. He pays me a lot of money and buys me lots of gifts, like this bike, in exchange.'

When I press her for the guy's name, she refuses to reveal it. However, she says I will definitely know him. 'Everyone knows who he is,' she says. 'He's won Oscars and is very well known. And everyone thinks he's happily married and a great family guy. If only they knew he's paying a young girl of 19 a lot of money to fuck his brains out.'

What I couldn't figure out is why she would tell a total stranger all this. It's almost as if she is proud of how clever she is, committing adultery and finding herself a sugar daddy to take care of her, and she needs to brag about this to somebody. Louise finally drops me off when I see a Tony Roma's restaurant on La Cienega. 'There's a kosher restaurant,' I shout.

Of course, their speciality is pork ribs, but I correctly calculate that Louise won't know the difference.

15

★ My Big Break ★

When I was hired to appear in *The Reagans*, it gave me one last glimmer of hope that my documentary could be salvaged – only to have that hope cruelly dashed. I had already resigned myself to editing the film into an offbeat royal romp through Hollywood instead of an insider's exposé when I receive a message from my new agent, Jacquie – who is based in Montreal and had been referred to me by a friend – telling me the casting director of a movie called *The Aviator*, about the early career of Howard Hughes, has seen my photo and has a part for me alongside Leonardo DiCaprio and Gwyneth Paltrow. (Paltrow was originally cast in the production but did not end up taking part.)

By this time, I wasn't terribly excited by such a phone call, figuring I would again be an extra or a stunt man or something equally insignificant.

But then Jacquie tells me the film is to be directed by Martin Scorsese and I start to get a little excited at the prospect of watching this legendary director in action. I actually got goosebumps when I heard the news. And furthermore, she informs me, I won't be a mere extra; I will actually play the role of a friend of Howard Hughes who visits the enigmatic billionaire while he is in the hospital recovering from a plane crash.

213

Holy crap, I think. Forget my documentary, I am going to actually appear in a Martin Scorsese film. Visions of Oscars dance in my head. How cool was this?

It turns out I still have to do a reading for the part, just to ensure I am breathing and literate, but Jacquie assures me it is just a formality. Sure enough, I read for about two minutes before the casting director sends me directly to wardrobe for a fitting and tells me to be on set the next day at 9 a.m. for an 11 a.m. shoot. Next I am given a contract, which specifies at least three days' work, as well as my first union credits.

I am practically pissing myself in fear of being discovered as a charlatan. Surely a great director like Scorsese can detect a fraud when he sees one. So I do what I usually do whenever I need to screw up my nerve – I rent *The Wizard of Oz* and fast-forward to the scene that never fails to inspire me, the part when the Cowardly Lion recites his immortal lines about courage and steels himself for the task ahead, taking on the Wicked Witch. That does the trick, though I am still very apprehensive.

When I arrive at the studio the next morning, the very first person I see is a guy walking a poodle who is a dead ringer for the actor Timothy Hutton, though I know Hutton isn't cast in *The Aviator*. (I later find out it was indeed Hutton, who was shooting the Johnny Depp film *Secret Window* on the adjoining lot.)

The studio is called Mel's Cité du Cinéma and is located near the Montreal waterfront. It is an enormous complex, resembling a First World War army camp, with tents set up outside for every phase of the operation, and which indeed operates with military-like precision.

First, I am sent off to hair. There must be at least 50 hair stylists in a tent, fixing the hair of various actors. My stylist, Michelle, gives me a trim, greases my hair a bit and makes me look more like Howard Hughes than DiCaprio himself, according to one onlooker.

Next is make-up. I tell the artist, as I always do before any TV interview, that I'm allergic to make-up, so I ask her to go light on the stuff. The truth is that I've always found it a complete pain in the ass trying to get the guck off my face when I'm finished.

Then I put on my suit and tie, and the black shoes that they assigned me the previous day. An assistant ushers me off to the set right away. Including me, there are six actors on set, including Jude Law, who seems rather quiet. He is probably as nervous as I am to be directed by Scorsese. A guy with a microphone announces 'Marty's arriving, Marty's arriving, get ready folks.' It is as if the President of the United States is about to arrive – except the President did not direct my favourite film of all time, *Goodfellas*, so this is even more momentous. Meanwhile, DiCaprio, playing Hughes, is in a hospital bed, all bandaged up, waiting for shooting to commence.

Scorsese sweeps in, introduces himself and asks me to call him 'Marty'. He has obviously been shuffling back and forth from scene to scene. *The Aviator* sets are huge and sometimes hundreds of actors will be on set just for one scene. In contrast, my scene is small. What impresses me about Scorsese is his simplicity and how he knows precisely what he wants. Within two minutes of meeting him, I feel like I've known the guy my entire life.

My line is simple. After Jude Law and Adam Goldberg deliver their lines, I am to look around and say, with concern, in the background, 'I hope he's OK. I think he'll be fine.' Every time I deliver it, I keep thinking the jig is up. Marty will catch on that I'm an imposter, and I'll be escorted unceremoniously off the set and heaved into the garbage cans in a nearby alley. But suddenly, we are finished. We only need three takes. Marty turns to me after we're done and says, 'Good work, Ian. You're a natural.' If he only knew it was my first time before a real camera. This business is not as difficult as it seemed.

I get a chance to talk to DiCaprio later in the day, when I notice

215

him smoking a cigarette with his girlfriend at the time, Brazilian supermodel Gisele Bündchen. (Later I spot the two of them making out behind a trailer.) He tells me he noticed me during my scene and thought I did a good job. He says he is quite impressed with the local actors from Montreal. 'And, by the way,' he says, after I address him as Mr DiCaprio, 'please call me Leo.'

He is a surprisingly nice guy. Considering that he may at the time be the number-one box-office star in the world, he appears completely normal. I tell him that I had a run-in about one of my books with the entertainment lawyer Rosemary Carroll, the ex-wife of Jim Carroll, the character he played in *The Basketball Diaries*, which results in a discussion of small independent films vs. Hollywood blockbusters. He tells me he actually preferred his life before *Titanic*, when he could go to a grocery store without being accosted. Although I was not blown away by his acting – I prefer the purists like Sir Laurence Olivier and Marlon Brando, and I didn't think Leo was anywhere near their league – the one thing that impresses me about him is his dedication, the effort he puts in, and the way he memorises his lines. During my subsequent days on the set, I notice that Leo always knows his lines inside out, unlike most of the other actors I had worked with to that point. On the set of *The Reagans*, James Brolin always carried his lines in his pocket and kept referring to them.

On another occasion, I have a chance to talk with Jude Law, who starts dishing the dirt to me and a female crew member on a variety of topics. I have a feeling he is trying to impress her and that he wouldn't be so forthcoming if she wasn't there. He tells us that Scorsese, DiCaprio and Alec Baldwin chipped in to hire a private caterer just for them 'while the rest of us have to eat the craft services swill'. Actually, the food is quite good. And he isn't really dissing those guys – he tells us that he is 'in awe' of Scorsese.

He says he couldn't believe Marty had cast DiCaprio as Hughes when he heard the news. 'At first, I thought it was a joke,' he tells us. 'Don't misunderstand, Leo's a great actor. I've watched *The Basketball Diaries*, like, eight times, but I couldn't imagine him playing Hughes. But, so far, he's really pulled it off. You have to give him credit.'

I steer the discussion to sports. It turns out that he's a huge fan of Tottenham, which I already know, and I tell him that I am considering going undercover as a football hooligan. I know Tottenham hooligans are particularly notorious and am actually hoping he can pull some strings with the club. But he is most unenthusiastic about the idea. 'You're taking your life in your hands,' he tells me. 'I wouldn't advise it. I don't know how good an actor you are, but you're not English and those lads will spot you in a minute.'

In my only conversation with Alec Baldwin, behind the trailers, I ask him for advice on how to make it in Hollywood and he tells me, 'Sometimes it's who you blow, sometimes it's who you know. But if you know who to blow, you've got an instant advantage when you're first coming up. Of course, that didn't help me because I was cursed with heterosexuality.' I tell him I had recently acted in a pilot with his brother, Billy, and that I think he is very underrated as an actor. He agrees and then confides that he prefers films to TV. 'You only have to work a few weeks and then you get to take a vacation,' he tells me. 'TV is hard work. I'd never want to do a series.' I think of that conversation a year later, when he is starring in the NBC comedy series *30 Rock*.

I am actually hoping to meet Kate Beckinsale, who is playing my old friend Ava Gardner in the film. I imagine I could share some insights with her about Ava. But I don't come across her, or any of the other big names who appear in the film, such as Cate Blanchett and Gwen Stefani. I did get to speak to Alan Alda a couple of times, because he was in one of my scenes, but it was nothing more than small talk.

The stars each have their own trailer, and I am dying to sneak aboard one to see what is inside, but I chicken out. There are actually security guards everywhere and they seem pretty vigilant.

The next few days are gruelling. I have to participate in the integral Senate hearing scene, though I have no lines. It is shot in the Montreal courthouse, where the heat of the lights and equipment make the place unbearable. One day, we shoot for 15 hours, with only a break for lunch in the sweltering 90-degree August heat. In this scene, I have to sit for hours on end while Leo and Alda deliver their lines through take after take. This is where I really get to see Scorsese do his thing, though the only person he really interacts with during the scene is DiCaprio. The director repeatedly takes him aside and gives him pointers, making suggestions or reading a particular line the way he wants Leo to deliver it. The first day seems to go on forever. Marty is never happy with the scene and it isn't until just before midnight that his assistant director tells us, 'Marty's checking the tape,' which means he wants to see how the scene looks before deciding if it's usable. Finally, he comes out a half-hour later and announces, 'It's a wrap.' Leo, who looks exhausted, bursts into a big smile and the few hundred people participating in the scene give him a standing ovation. Everyone is delighted to finally go home.

The only good thing about the exhausting schedule is the money. My contract doesn't specify how much I will be paid for appearing in the film, because the amount is based on union rates and depends on how many hours I am needed, how much overtime, etc. In the end, I make several thousand dollars, which I use to purchase a new sax.

It isn't until my final day on the set that I realise just how elaborate the production has been when one of the actors, Michael Maloley, tells me about some of the behind-the-scenes goings-on. He says the ballroom scene had a big band and about 1,000 extras. He guesses that this scene alone must have cost millions. He played a photographer in the scene. Michael ends up spending a couple of months on the set of *The Aviator*. 'I've played so many different characters – from a photographer to a dancer, to one of Leo's entourage. If anyone notices, I'm probably the star of this whole show. The problem is, I look different in every scene,' he says.

The last time I talk to Leo is on the second-to-last day of the Senate hearing. He says how thankful he is to the city for donating the courtroom. 'They gave it to Marty as a gift for shooting in Montreal,' he explains. 'I thought that was really nice.'

While Scorsese is in town, various sources call me providing info on his whereabouts, including sightings of the director shopping downtown for shoes and eating in a number of different restaurants. Everyone who sees him has the same first impression as me – 'He's so short.'

One day, a friend calls to tell me that the owner of Mythos Restaurant had just phoned, telling him that Scorsese was dining there that night. He offers to seat my friend and I at a table right beside the director.

Donning a pair of shades, but not my His Highness outfit – I didn't want to stand out, after all – we sit beside Marty and his dining companion, a woman in her early 50s, and eavesdrop for a couple of hours. Little did Marty know that one of his actors was hanging on every word he said. Scorsese talked mainly about blues music, which made sense because, unbeknownst to me, his next project was a series on the history of the blues.

I had finally achieved my goal and landed a role in a genuine Hollywood film. Yet suddenly my own film didn't seem very important any more. The irony was not lost on me. I had set out to expose Hollywood celebrity culture and had many eye-opening experiences along the way; yet my brief few days acting alongside the world's most famous actor and one of history's legendary directors had given me a taste of real Hollywood glamour and I wanted more. I no longer wanted to blow the lid off Hollywood. Now, I wanted to be part of it.

I actually felt kind of bad for all the actors I had followed for months whose Hollywood dreams had turned to despair, while I had set out to audition for a lark and been cast in two movies, including one of the top blockbusters of the decade. It didn't seem very fair.

But that's showbiz. There's something very Darwinian about the whole thing, I figured. If Hollywood success is about the survival of the fittest, then so be it. I was just a bit fitter than the others, I concluded smugly.

A few months later, I fly back to LA and meet up with my cameraman, Miles, to film what I figure will be the climactic scene of my documentary: me, stepping up on the red carpet with my new buddies DiCaprio, Law, Scorsese, Blanchett et al. at the premiere of *The Aviator* at Grauman's Chinese Theater in Hollywood.

This time, I do not don my green shirt and gold bow tie, but a tux. It no longer seems fitting to thumb my nose at the business that had welcomed me with open arms, that had embraced me so warmly. This evening will be the start of something big. Maybe I will chat with Marty on our way out about what he might have for me in his next picture. After all, I hear that he had already signed Leo for another film. I assume we were now one big happy family.

And though I had only one line, I delivered it with such grace that I am sure to be noticed. Perhaps a best supporting actor Oscar is a little unrealistic this time around, but in the next film, who knows?

I had considered renting a limousine for my grand entrance, but when I saw what they were charging, I figured that you couldn't drive a limo up on the red carpet anyway. So Miles and I walk. When we arrive at the roped-off entrance, the crowds are assembled to see us stars arrive. I saunter up to the tuxedo-clad security guy manning the ropes.

'Ian Halperin,' I announce casually.

'What about him?' comes the reply.

'That's me. I'm here for the premiere.'

'You got an invitation?'

'No, but check the list.'

'There is no list. You don't have an invitation and I didn't see you in the movie. You're not getting in.' (YouTube)

In the distance, I spot Marty and Leo milling about on the red carpet, posing for the paparazzi and waving to the crowd.

'Marty,' I yell out. 'Over here, they won't let me in.' He doesn't even look over.

'Leo, it's me!' I shout. DiCaprio briefly looks my way, shows no sign of recognition, and quickly turns back to the publicist by his side. Then I see my fellow documentary film-maker, Michael Moore, milling about on the red carpet. What the hell is he doing here? That fat bastard's not even in the film.

A few weeks later, I finally get the chance to see the film at a local multiplex. My hospital scene has been cut completely. I think there is a fleeting glimpse of my elbow in the courthouse Senate hearing scene.

First *The Reagans* gets axed by CBS and now this. I must be under some kind of Hollywood curse. There's no business like show business.

The project was complete, dismal failure though it may have been. But there was still one piece of unfinished business – an unkept promise. Before I leave Los Angeles, I send my friend Elissa to one of the many tacky tourist shops that line Hollywood Boulevard to make an important purchase.

When I arrive back in Montreal, I immediately drive to the cemetery where my mother is buried. Stopping at her grave, I remove from its bag the recent purchase – a perfect replica of an Oscar statue – and place it on her headstone.

'Best Mom' the inscription reads.

EPILOGUE

★ The End ★

When the documentary was finally finished, it had become the most gruelling project I'd ever worked on. I now knew more about Hollywood than I'd ever hoped for and had experienced first-hand what it was like to reach for the dream, only to be chewed up and spat out like so many thousands of hopeful actors.

When I submitted the finished project to CTV, which had commissioned the doc in the first place, they were bemused. They had hired me to document the plight of Canadian actors trying to make it during pilot season. Instead, I had unilaterally decided to turn the film into a self-serving undercover piece documenting my own experiences. They informed me they weren't going to air it. Their rejection was almost as heartbreaking as being left on *The Aviator* cutting-room floor. It meant that two years of agony, transcontinental flights, sweat and occasional humiliation had all been for nothing, not to mention sometimes being unable to see my baby daughter for weeks at a time. After the network formally rejected the film and signed a contract assigning me full rights and ownership, I actually returned to LA twice more at my own expense, but it appeared to be a fool's errand.

The film languished on the shelf for what seemed like forever until I caught a break. In the interval between the time I started my

223

film and its completion, a global phenomenon had occurred under the name of Borat. Sacha Baron Cohen's film had demonstrated the mass appeal of a whole new film genre, the mockumentary, which revealed greater insight about its subjects than a traditional doc. A number of people who had seen my finished film actually remarked on the similarity of some of His Highness's stunts to those of Borat, Cohen's hilarious alter ego, who poses as a Kazakh journalist to uncover the secrets of America.

Most of my His Highness scenes were actually shot long before *Borat* was released and, besides, they couldn't even hold a candle to the pure genius of Baron Cohen. But one day I received a call from an unlikely source. The man identified himself as Joe Franklin, media consultant of the Laugh Factory, the world's largest comedy club, located in New York's Times Square. The club was opening up a new state-of-the-art movie theatre and they wanted to book my film for an extended run.

'You're going to be the next Borat,' Franklin tells me as he ushers me into his office. But I'm hardly paying attention because my eyes are immediately riveted to the walls, which are covered floor to ceiling with photos of Franklin and a who's who of Hollywood celebrities. There are signed photos of Franklin with everybody from Marilyn Monroe to Elvis Presley, from Frank Sinatra and John Lennon to countless US presidents.

'How do you know all these people?' I ask him.

He reaches for a book. It's the *Guinness Book of World Records*. There, among the world's tallest human and various other freaks is Joe Franklin, billed as the 'most durable talk-show host', with more than 31,000 episodes.

'I was the first,' he tells me.

It seems that Franklin hosted the world's first-ever TV talk show, the *Joe Franklin Show*, which ran from 1950 to 1997 on WABC TV. But that's not what impressed me the most.

Franklin was actually responsible for introducing a number of future superstars on his show, including a couple of young New Yorkers named Barbra Streisand and Woody Allen, not to mention Liza Minelli and Bill Cosby, as well as a still obscure Elvis Presley, who made his TV debut on Franklin's show long before he appeared on *Ed Sullivan*. Franklin also played himself in the Allen films *Broadway Danny Rose* and *Manhattan*, as well as in *Ghostbusters*.

In the next hour, I learn more about Hollywood than I had in the last three years. (YouTube)

'I invented the talk TV format,' he tells me. 'I invented it when I was a kid. I was choosing records for a guy named Martin Block on a show called *The Make Believe Ballroom* and they asked me if I'd like to do an hour a day on Channel 7. They said, "Joe, what would you like to do?" I said just people talking eyeball to eyeball. They said, "Joe, you're out of your mind – a talk show on television would not work, you need action." Then I said what about kids dancing to records. They said, "You're crazy." Then Dick Clark becomes a billionaire. But I defied them; I did the first TV talk show of its kind and, believe me, talk shows are here to stay.'

He estimates that he's interviewed more than 300,000 people on radio and television in the last 50 years. He starts to list all the memorable guests he's had on his show over the years and it's like a who's who of twentieth-century history and popular culture – Frank Sinatra, Michael Jackson, Muhammad Ali, John F. Kennedy and four other US presidents, Humphrey Bogart, John Lennon, Groucho Marx . . . the list goes on and on.

'The only one I never had was Greta Garbo,' he says. 'She was unavailable, so to speak. Greta was timeless, frozen in time.'

There's Marilyn Monroe memorabilia all over the office, so I ask Franklin if he knew her.

'Did I know her? I was one of her best friends,' he tells me. 'We collaborated on a book together called *The Marilyn Monroe Story* in

1953 when I was only 27. It sells now for $8,000 on eBay. I met her on a radio show called *Luncheon at Sardis*. The book I did with Marilyn was a puff piece, but her work was supreme.'

'What was she like?' I ask.

'She was sweet, fiercely intelligent and bright. She didn't even need a lawyer to handle her affairs. When she died, she was probably done in by certain political people because she was too close, knew too many secrets.'

I couldn't resist asking the question that had been on my mind since he started talking about her in a tone that implied more than a friendship.

'Did you sleep with her?'

'A gentleman doesn't talk about those things,' he replies with a twinkle in his eye.

I ask him to talk about some of the other memorable guests on his show.

'Marlon Brando. Brando revolutionised acting. Sinatra was on my show four times; there will never be another. He loved Ava Gardner – she got a screen test passed without ever saying a word because he loved her.'

And then he brings up a Hollywood figure that I can't seem to shake, even though he's been dead for three decades.

'I had Chaplin on my show in 1972, when he got his award at the Lincoln Center. He was interesting. He told me he had people analyse all the Freudian meanings of his movies. Every time he kicked the fat man's behind, they thought he had other intentions. Chaplin did not. He just wanted to make people laugh.'

He describes Woody Allen as Chaplin's natural successor. 'Woody got his first big exposure on my show; I discovered him, too. He's a modern day Charlie Chaplin, no getting around it. He's a genius.'

I ask him how today's Hollywood compares with the old days.

'Every day in Hollywood is crazy,' he says. 'Just the budgets – the fact that a movie has a $35 million budget and $1 million is allotted just for dope. You can see it in the movie, which is terrible, when it looks like the whole cast and crew is on dope.

'A lot of Hollywood is fraud. I would not make it today because I'm too nice. Today, it's too mean-spirited.'

I tell Franklin about my poker game with the Queers of the Round Table and ask him whether he thinks most actors are really as gay as they claim.

'Hollywood's full of secrets – who went out with who, who's sleeping with who, which men are gay, which women are lesbians,' he replies. 'I think at least one of four male actors today in Hollywood is gay, and the other three are half-gay. It's not good for their public image because people want to see them be males: virile, all man.'

I tell him about my discussion with Michael Pattinson and ask him if he's heard anything about Scientology trying to convert gay actors to heterosexuality, but Franklin believes much of the information being spread about the Church is malicious.

'Scientology is a worthwhile movement,' he insists. 'Tom Cruise is very active. I'm not sure about Travolta being gay – John's a big ladies' man.'

Franklin was once a stand-up comedian on the Borscht Belt circuit, and it shows as he tells one corny joke after another.

'The secret ingredient in Hollywood is sincerity,' he says. 'Once you learn how to fake that, you've got it made.'

I ask him if he was ever pressured not to interview certain actors during the blacklist.

'Most of that came before my show was on the air, in the '50s,' he explains. But he maintains that the blacklist never really ended, it just took a different form.

'There are secret unwritten blacklists today,' he says, 'but nothing like the old days, when it broke many hearts. Common sense, we hope, will prevail.'

Coincidentally, I had recently seen the movie *The Aristocrats*, where some of the world's best-known comedians tell their version of the most notorious and disgusting joke ever told – a joke that heretofore comedians only told amongst themselves. The film is actually hysterically funny, not to mention quite disturbing.

The most infamous scene just happens to be a segment where the comedienne Sarah Silverman, while telling her version of the joke, looks straight into the camera and, in a deadpan tone, says, 'Joe Franklin Raped Me.' It was obviously meant to be part of the joke and was just one of the hundreds of over-the-top, made-up moments in the film. But Franklin was not amused, and I can hardly blame him.

'I didn't find that particularly funny,' he says. 'Today's movies have got more profanity, less censorship; in fact, no censorship. In the old days, there were rules, common sense prevailed, you could not say "pregnant", you had to say "with child". Today the flavour is horror stuff.'

I ask him to name the best movie he's seen this year and he cites *Borat*.

'*Borat* is a new kind of technique, interactive – everyone gets involved in a picture like that,' he says. Then he throws me for a loop. 'Don't worry, you'll be bigger.'

What does he mean by that, I ask.

'We need someone to shake this town up,' he responds. 'I haven't had a Jew break since Woody. In fact, New York hasn't had someone since Seinfeld. What a mitzvah, His Highness has arrived, blue eyes, big nose, black hair and all.'

I'm thinking this is part of his schtick and that he's having a bit of fun at my expense, but he seems to be all business, then I remember I'm actually here to talk about promoting my film, *His Highness Hollywood*.

'I like you very much because you have a great look, very marketable,' he continues. 'I guarantee you're going to fly. Your motivation should be your pay cheque and you'll be OK. You're going to be a star; you're the next big thing. Just don't let it get to your head. You pay attention – you don't look into my belly button or nose, you look into my eyeballs. You're going to make it, kid.'

Then one of America's legendary television personalities makes me a proposition. He tells me he's been approached by countless TV stations since *The Joe Franklin Show* ended a few years ago. He's been doing a national radio talk show since then, but he misses TV. He wants me to host a show with him.

'I think the two of us can have a great show together. I'd love to be with you. We'd be another Olson and Johnson, Abbott and Costello. Lets do it.' (YouTube)

I can't quite believe my ears. Woody Allen, Barbra Streisand, Elvis Presley . . . Ian Halperin?

I just hope he doesn't tape me.

229

POSTSCRIPT

Shortly after the publication of this book in America, I became the
focus of a series of articles on New York's biggest blog, Gawker.com.
My book seemed to capture the imaginations of the liberal-minded
folks at Gawker, in contrast to the persecution I was receiving online.
One member of the Church of Scientology emailed me saying he was
going to make online posts calling for a boycott of the book and at
the other end of the spectrum there were threats from unidentified
individuals. I received several intimidating phone calls at my Midtown
apartment in Manhattan. One of them scared the living daylights out
of me. 'Back off if you enjoy breathing,' the husky voice at the other
end of the line said.

I decided to retreat to the woods of Canada until things
quietened down. But getting out of my apartment building to head
for LaGuardia Airport was not an easy task. The associate editor
of Defamer.com – Gawker's LA sister website – had written that
I intended to go into hiding and the media had reacted. Numerous
camera crews from all over the world were camped in front of my
building hoping to get my side of the story. A car was waiting for
me outside. Dressed in sunglasses and a red wool hat, I exited to
the blinding flashes of cameras. One photographer from Brazil was

trampled in the crush and got badly bruised. It was the longest 20 yards of my life. Finally, I made it into the car, en route for my home town, Montreal. I spent weeks up in the mountains a couple of hours north of the city waiting till I felt safe enough to return to New York.

Meanwhile, I was putting the finishing touches to my documentary *His Highness Hollywood*. Then the president of one of New York's most prestigious arts venues contacted me about screening my film at the National Arts Club. Aldon James is one of the most powerful people on the city's art scene. He offered to throw an open-bar-and-buffet reception for 200 people before the screening. I would have been a fool to refuse his offer, so I booked a flight back to New York to prepare for the grand opening.

Soon, I was in the grip of a familiar anxiety about how my film would be greeted. On the night, I showed up at the National Arts Club and the manager told me that demand was so high that there weren't enough seats in the place. 'We've had over 300 calls to get in,' he said. 'We've added as many seats as we can but still there's going to be a lot of people who won't get in.' I thought to myself that this could only be the best of my problems. An overcrowded house at an opening is every artist's dream.

As the people piled in, I noticed several members of New York's media and a couple of TV crews. Some film-industry people also showed up, including the head of acquisitions at Sony, Seth Horowitz. A few supermodels who were friends from my old days undercover as a male model also turned up. Then one of the world's most famous authors appeared. Andrew Morton, Princess Diana's confidant and biographer, who had just written a scathing *New York Times* No. 1 bestseller on Tom Cruise, sauntered in. I was surprised by how tall Morton was. I had seen him on television several times but had no idea he was 6 ft 6 in. Dawn Olsen, the editor of the popular celebrity blog site Glosslip.com, introduced me to Morton. We started talking about our books, the focus being on Scientology and the rumours about Tom Cruise's sexuality. In his book, Morton insists that Cruise is not gay and I've never seen any proof that he is, either.

When everyone was seated and legendary New York radio talk-show host and Rock 'n' Roll Hall of Fame inductee Joey Reynolds had introduced the evening, the room went dark. The film started. I breathed a sigh of relief but four minutes later the most stressful and bizarre incident of my career took place. The house lights came back on and there was panic around the area where the film projector was located. The film was frozen and the head technician, Gregory Singer, had no idea why it had happened. He said he had done a test run a couple of hours before the event and everything had worked. He was baffled.

After a two-hour delay, we had to decide what to do. No one had left. In fact, most of the patrons that night seemed ecstatic about the delay, which meant they could take greater advantage of the free bar and the buffet. 'I'm having the time of my life,' a writer from *Vanity Fair* told me. 'Even if you can't get the film rolling again, the night has been fun. And no one will forget it.'

Finally, Singer came up to me and said that the only solution would be to show an old cut of the film on a DVD player that would project onto the screen. I agreed. My agent warned the audience that they would be seeing a rough cut. Still, the reaction seemed very positive. 'It's like *Borat* but a bit more sophisticated,' said Andrew Morton. 'I see big potential here. It'll be interesting to see the final cut.'

The next day, I got a call from Singer telling me that he had finished doing tests to determine what had happened. 'Definitely sabotage,' he said. 'I tested the system before the screening and everything was clean. Now I've found 12 viruses. While I was at dinner, someone obviously infected the projection system with viruses. Someone didn't want your film to be screened.'

Convinced that he was right, I leaked the story to Dawn Olsen at Glosslip. After her post, my phone once again began ringing off the hook. The *New York Post*'s high-profile gossip section 'Page Six' mentioned the incident in a piece about celebrities terminating their links to the Church. Many people were asking whether someone linked to the Church of Scientology might have been behind the technical difficulties. Although I had no proof that the Church had tried to stop the film being shown, I was highly suspicious. Still, I was no nearer to the bottom of it all, as it could have been anyone – someone out simply to cause havoc.

I decided to spend the time until the official release of my film in autumn 2008 in the sanctuary of my Canadian home in the mountains. It wasn't as if I wouldn't have anything to do. The research for my next book (about going undercover as a paparazzo following Britney Spears) was complete, so I would spend the next few months in the mountains writing it all up. I made sure to back everything up several times, just in case someone caught wind of where I was and tried to infect my laptop.

In Canada, I received a call from someone purporting to be a former Scientologist informing me that I was on the Church's radar. He claimed that the folks at Scientology were planning on spending millions of dollars trying to discredit the recent wave of negative publicity, which included my book, Morton's book and an online campaign by a group of people calling themselves Anonymous, who stated that they were out to 'expel Scientology from the Internet' because of what they saw as the Church's long history of corruption. The caller told me that the Church was very nervous about the release of my upcoming film. 'A lot of their key celebrities are donating millions of dollars to stop the siege of bad publicity,' the source said. 'It's the only way they might be able to stop all the terrible press they've been receiving. I don't think you're in danger but I strongly suggest you keep all the details about your film secret until it's released.'

I had no idea how seriously to take the caller's advice, but I decided to take no risks. I made 14 back-up copies of all the footage and the final cut. I stored them in several locations in Canada, the US and at a close friend's home in Switzerland.

I hope the people at the Church realise that my book and film are not part of any kind of vendetta against them. In fact, I go out of my way to say positive things about the religion in both the book and the film. However, I do feel that it should take to heart and address some of the criticism. During my time undercover at the Church of Scientology, I met many terrific, nice people. Hopefully, they and others like them will push for change and, in the end, good will come out of the current debate surrounding Scientology.